GASA GASA GIRL GOES TO CAMP

WINTER 9L, WATERCOLOR, 22 BY 30 INCHES.

Gasa Gasa Girl Goes to Camp

A Nisei Youth behind a World War II Fence

Lily Yuriko Nakai Havey

foreword by Cherstin Lyon

THE UNIVERSITY OF UTAH PRESS
Salt Lake City

TANNER TRUST FUND
Special Collections, J. Willard Marriott Library

Publication of this book is made possible in part by a generous grant
from the Tanner Trust Fund, Special Collections, J. Willard Marriott Library.
The publisher gratefully acknowledges this contribution.

The Defiance House Man colophon is a registered trademark
of the University of Utah Press. It is based on a four-foot-tall
Ancient Puebloan pictograph (late PIII) near Glen Canyon, Utah.

18 17 16 15   2 3 4 5

LIBRARY OF CONGRESS CATALOGING-IN-PUBLICATION DATA
Havey, Lily Yuriko Nakai, 1932-
  Gasa-gasa girl goes to camp : a Nisei youth behind a World War II fence
/ Lily Yuriko Nakai Havey ; foreword by Cherstin Lyon.
    pages cm
  ISBN 978-1-60781-343-9 (hardback)
  ISBN 978-1-60781-345-3 (ebook)
1. Havey, Lily Yuriko Nakai, 1932 —Childhood and youth. 2. Japanese
Americans—Evacuation and relocation, 1942-1945. 3. Granada Relocation
Center—History. 4. World War, 1939-1945—Concentration
camps—Colorado—Amache. 5. Japanese Americans—Biography. 6. Japanese
American women—Biography. I. Title.
  D769.8.A6H384 2014
  940.53'1778898092—dc23
  [B]
                                2013043810

Frontispiece: Winter 9L, watercolor, 22 by 30 inches

Printed and bound in Malaysia.

I dedicate this work to my mother and father
and all the pioneering Issei without whom this book
would contain only blank pages.

Contents

Foreword

Lily Yuriko Nakai Havey, a Nisei, was caught between two cultures, the American one into which she was born and the Japanese one that her parents carried with them when they immigrated to the United States. Lily explains:

> As with many of the second-generation children, I internalized the principles of *gaman* and *shikataganai* at an early age, learning not to verbalize fears, frustration, and confusion. We learned to "suck it in." Stoic and principled Japanese were supposed to handle unbearable situations in this manner. At long last—realizing that the trauma of the war years continually hampered healthy emotional development—I have given myself permission to "let it hang out" and express these emotions through my paintings and stories.

Lily's journey into the emotions and memories of her past is a poignant example of the power of historical memory. History, especially when it is marked by trauma, is not something that just happens and is recorded in all of its factual detail. Historical memory evolves and becomes even more meaningful over time.

This book is much more than a record of one girl's wartime experiences shaped by her family's forced removal from California and indefinite incarceration in the remote southeastern corner of Colorado. It provides an opportunity for readers to share Lily's journey into the recesses of her own memory, even into the nightmares of her past. Photographs document the harsh living conditions and resiliency of Japanese Americans during their wartime incarceration in prison camps, but Lily's paintings open up a different world to us, a world depicting a child's fears and longings and an adult's attempt to recover some of what was lost during those years.

Numerous books document the historical events that led to Lily's personal trauma. On February 19, 1942, after the bombing of Pearl Harbor by the Japanese military, President Franklin Roosevelt signed Executive Order 9066 and set in motion a series of unforgettable events forcing the removal and incarceration of 120,000 individuals of Japanese descent for what appeared to be the duration of the war. Nakai family members were ordered to abandon their livelihoods and home in the spring of 1942 and relocated from their western coastal community into one of ten "internment" camps built in California, Arizona, Utah, Idaho, Wyoming, Colorado, and Arkansas. Even though the Supreme Court in 1944 bowed to the military in a wartime ruling that race-based curfews and exclusion orders for all persons of Japanese descent from the West Coast and lower third of Arizona were constitutional, it recognized at the same time—in the separate case of *Ex parte Mitsuye Endo*—that it was not within the government's powers to hold citizens without due process. Hence, the entire internment program was a manifestation of racism.

During the 1980s, the Ninth Circuit Court of Appeals and Congress agreed that the wartime removal had not been constitutional. The Ninth Circuit Court overturned the wartime convictions of Gordon Hirabayashi, Minoru Yasui, and Fred Korematsu, whose case had led to the previous upholding of Japanese exclusion. Congress concluded that the forced removal and incarceration of Japanese Americans had been the result of wartime hysteria, racial prejudice, and a failure of leadership and recommended not only an apology but also reparation for financial harm incurred during the war. It was only after President Reagan offered a formal apology in 1988 that many Japanese Americans were able to absolve their feelings of guilt for having been locked up in a kind of prison and, by implication, having done something wrong.

As did many former internees, Lily went back to see the place where she had spent so many of her formative years, the place where she had transitioned from a child to a young woman, but she returned only after she had started her personal journey of remembering. When the United States entered the war, Lily was barely ten years old. She spent almost four years, first imprisoned at the Santa Anita Assembly Center in Pasadena, California, and then—after transport by train—at the Amache Relocation Center (also known as the Granada Relocation Center) in Colorado. These years of confinement coincided with her transformative years of puberty, leaving an indelible mark on Lily that she later sought to reconcile through her artwork and process of remembering.

As Lily writes, this book is not meant to be a factual record of everything that marked the wartime experiences of 120,000 individuals who were caught in a tragic display of intolerance and racial prejudice. It is an artistically written record of one woman's journey into her past. Lily acknowledges that a few of her memories were recreated from dreams and some details were added to fill in the gaps of her memory.

Internationally renowned oral historian and theorist Alessandro Portelli has published extensively on the errors and revisions that mark all historical memory. Instead of dismissing historical memories for their flaws, Portelli has urged researchers and others to look at memory differently. What leads individuals to reshape their memories of the past in particular ways—to remember some things quite clearly and revise other memories—is precisely what makes studying memory so important. All history is constructed from fragments of an imperfectly documented and remembered past.

Other scholars, such as Michael Kammen, emphasize how important historical amnesia is in constructing all historical memory. What we remember is only a fragmented remainder of what we have forgotten. Lily's desire to reconstruct her memories, first in the form of paintings and later as narrative, only became possible—and I might say imperative—after the passage of time.

The stories and images that fill this book are significant for many reasons. We have few historical accounts of women's distinctive experiences in the camps, especially those of young women going through puberty. In this book, we get a rare glimpse into the ways camp life affected Lily's education about sexuality and her body. Even though the story is narrated through the voice of a young person, the flashbacks into her mother's formative years in

Japan and reaction to camp confinement are surely the result of adult reflections on the parallels linking the lives of mother and daughter. The guilt that Lily's mother carried—which helps explain why she suffered as a child and again as a mother during wartime—comes to us secondhand but can help readers think more deeply about the ways in which Issei women suffered and yet found opportunities for self-discovery in the camp environment. In her touching reflections on her father's inability to cope with the confinement and his lack of purpose in the camp, Lily also constructs a complex explanation for the seeming disintegration of family structure and Issei authority in camp.

The great value of this book is that it intimately shares one woman's memories of the past and, at the same time, is able to explore issues rarely discussed in any historical or narrative literature about the camp experience, particularly for women.

CHERSTIN LYON
California State University, San Bernardino

Preface

I am a Japanese American artist. Along with 120,000 other Japanese Americans, I was incarcerated in an American concentration camp during World War II. In the 1980s, I learned about armed-service personnel suffering from post-traumatic stress disorder (PTSD) and wondered whether some of my unease with confined spaces—being boxed in—bright lights, and loud noises might be symptoms of the same syndrome. I painted a series of watercolors about my experiences at the Santa Anita Assembly Center and the Amache Relocation Center in Colorado.

Because we were forbidden to have cameras until 1945, toward the end of our stay in camp, I have no photos of myself between the ages of ten and thirteen. For this reason, I did not attempt to include a "real" self in my paintings but, rather, fabricated fictional/fantasy characters. I was not aware that our camp actually had had a photographic studio established in August 1944, where I might have had my portrait taken.

At a number of exhibitions of my paintings, the curators asked me to write short descriptions of the art. Most of my paintings are not concrete images of the camps but instead express my personal reactions and feelings about my experience. When I began to write, however, I found that one paragraph was hardly sufficient to explain them. I expanded the captions, and more words, more feelings, streamed out. I could not stop. This book is the result.

I am primarily a visual person. I wrote the stories as snapshots of what I saw and heard. It was as if I held a movie camera at the scene and recorded the events. The result is a series of miniscenes, rather than a single narrative. The stories are roughly in chronological order from the initial assembly at Santa Anita to the closing days at Amache.

Most of the paintings and the accompanying stories are based on memories more than sixty years old. When I couldn't remember details, I added creative embellishments. A few are dream fragments. For significant events and dates, I did research at the Japanese American National Museum in Los Angeles, the National Archives, and the J. Willard Marriott Library at the University of Utah. I have given aliases to some people still living. All the stories about my mother are true, as far as I can recall her telling them to me.

My paintings and stories have been healing and cathartic. Sharing my stories and showing my paintings have built a sense of lightness and freedom.

GASA GASA GIRL GOES TO CAMP

LONGING, WATERCOLOR, 22 BY 30 INCHES.
An Ichimatsu doll is a one-of-a-kind item treasured by successive generations.
In my painting, it represents the unobtainable: freedom. This doll is based on one photographed
in Ningy: *The Art of the Japanese Doll* by Alan Scott Pate.

Camping at Santa Anita

ARCADIA, NO. 1

"You're lucky." That's what everyone told us. Horse stables…that's where they billeted the first wave of evacuees from the West Coast. By the time my family—my mother, my father, my brother, and I—arrived at the Santa Anita Racetrack, renamed the Assembly Center, there were makeshift tar-paper barracks. We lived in one of those. Some people lived in the horse stables.

Lucky? That's what we were told. So where did the horses go to live? Were they, too, lucky? It was temporary, the people in charge said. Temporary turned into six months. After that, when we were moved again, it got worse, much worse. Temporary became permanent. On the fateful morning we gathered in front of a church in March of 1942, I knew an ominous event was unfolding but had scant knowledge of its historical significance.

"*Koko de mat'tete, ne, Yuri-chan,*" my mother entreats. "Wait here."

"I'll be all alone. Let me come. Let me come. Please," I beg.

"No. Sit quietly," she insists in Japanese; I always answer her in English. "Where's Daddy?"

"I don't know. I have to register."

"Where's Sumiya? How come he doesn't have to just sit around?"

"That's OK. He's a boy. He can take care of himself."

"That's OK, that's OK, he's a boy," I mutter loudly enough for her to hear. How many times have I heard that before? A million?

TOWERS OF ARCADIA, WATERCOLOR, 22 BY 30 INCHES.
Santa Anita Assembly Center, the temporary camp where we were placed before being sent to Amache,
was in Arcadia, California. Arcadia was a place of peace and simplicity in ancient Greece; our barracks camp
was anything but. This painting expresses my bewilderment at my imprisonment. A church in the upper right corner
displays a gold cross, offering a glimmer of hope.

"Sit still. I'll be back soon." My mother hurries away.

I have just turned ten, and I am sitting on my father's cardboard suitcase because a month before, on February 19, 1942, President Roosevelt had signed Executive Order 9066. My mother explained that now we had to go somewhere inland to a camp. We'd ride a train and go to camp. Just imagine! A train ride to camp! I was so excited; how could I sit still? I'd never ridden a train. Boy Scouts and Girl Scouts camped in tents, built fires, roasted hot dogs, and told ghost stories after dark.

At camp my father and I could hike together, although he had warned, "No promises." When he and Sumiya went fishing, I'd ask to go, too, but my father scoffed, saying, "Fishing is for boys." Sometimes they came home without any fish, but neither of them seemed to care. They had the day together, and that seemed enough for them. No one I knew had ever camped because Japanese kids didn't belong to scouts; scouting was for white kids. I'd be the first in my group. I'd come back and tell Aiko and Helen, "My father and I hiked to a lake. He taught me to fish." I'd be so proud.

But where is the train my mother promised? Only a line of ordinary buses stretches down the street. This is bor…ing.

I scan the crowd for my father and brother. The men sport hats and ties. The women are gussied up in fancy clothes. My mother insisted I wear my white Sunday dress with red buttons and my black patent-leather shoes.

"This is a special trip," my mother said. "We must look neat. We don't want people to think we're beggars." Did people camp in good Sunday clothes? They'd get so dirty. And everyone looks so serious, so worried. Some women are crying. I want to say to them, "Hey, we're off on an adventure! Don't cry. It's going to be fun; you'll see."

I look up at the steeple. What's there, a cross? *I remember a cross swinging from the neck of a stern-faced woman dressed in black—an image somehow connected to a song: "Jesus loves me; this I know…" That's odd. "Jesus loves me; this I know, for the Bible tells me so." Jesus? The Bible?*

We're Buddhists and don't have a Bible. Where did this song come from? I vaguely recall a woman who grabbed my hand and led me through a huge

18286, WATERCOLOR, 22 BY 30 INCHES.
This was our family identification number during the war.

double door to where my mother waited. Now I'm waiting for my mother at a place strangely similar. Life is all mixed up.

My mother returns with cardboard tags stamped 18286 and ties one to the front of my dress; she puts another on my father's suitcase.

"What's this?" I ask.

"So many people; it's easier to remember numbers, so they gave us this number."

"That's funny. I'll write my name on it."

"No. They want only that number."

"You said we were going on a train."

"My mistake. Later we'll go on a train."

"Mama, I remember a lady."

"What lady?"

"The one with the cross."

"What are you talking about?"

"A long time ago there was a lady with a cross around her neck. She opened a big door, and you were waiting for me."

Just then a woman in the same sort of black robe walks into the church. "Look," I point. "It was a lady like her."

However, by the time my mother looks, the woman has disappeared. She simply says, "It's time to get on the bus, Yuriko."

"Where's Daddy?"

"He'll be here. Get in line."

"No, let's wait. Please. Let's wait for Daddy."

My brother appears just as we board the bus, but there is no sign of my father. I don't want people to see my underpants so I want to go last, but the crowd urges us up the steps. My mother pushes me forward. I insist on a window seat. Maybe I'll catch a glimpse of my father.

But the bus starts without him. My mother frowns and lays her hand on my forehead. "You feel hot. I'll go find some water."

I wait for a long time, and then I must have slept because the next thing I know, the bus has stopped. Outside I see soldiers in front of a barbed-wire fence, and behind them are row after row of black shacks but no tents.

Where are the tents? The mountains, the trees? So many boxes, suitcases, black-haired people. Who are they all? Are they all camping with us?

A small boy on the ground looks up and makes a face. I stick my tongue out at him.

"Yuriko," my mother warns, "sit still and be good."

"He did it first."

"You don't need to copy that bad boy."

No, I think, *but I could be bad here. Look at all these strangers. No one knows me. I don't know them. I could make all the faces I want. I could pinch babies' cheeks until they cry. Aiko does that; so could I. I could scuff my Sunday shoes, dirty my white dress, yell and scream at anyone I choose. What a camp that would be! No bossy "sit still," "chew your food," "practice," "hurry."*

"Yuriko, come, stand up." My mother nudges me forward. My suitcase is too heavy, so I drag it down the aisle. "Don't do that. The bottom will wear out," she scolds me.

I kick the suitcase out the door and jump off the bus. The ground feels wobbly. "Mama, let's go back home. I don't want to camp anymore. Let's find Daddy and go home."

A man at the gate calls out, "Get in line; get in line." After a long wait, we find ourselves before a man at a table. "Nakai. Go to Barrack 34, Room 6, Avenue N, by the Orange Mess."

He sounds like a robot. Orange mess? What's that? A pile of orange garbage? What are these mess tickets?

"Is this our camp?" I ask Mama. "How is Daddy going to find us?"

"This is a different kind of camp. For Japanese people," my mother explains.

"What do you mean?"

"That's what the government decided."

I trudge behind my mother and brother, dragging my suitcase, hoping the bottom will really fall apart. Barrack 34 looks exactly like all the others.

My mother and brother hurry into Room 6. No, I'm not going inside this dirty-looking building. I put down my suitcase and sit on it. I hate camping.

"The buildings are black. They're ugly," I grumble.

"It's tar paper, dummy," my brother yells out the door.

"Yuriko, you can't sit there all day," my mother admonishes. "Inside. Now!"

My mother takes my suitcase. I peek into the room: four metal beds. Striped gray mattresses. Ugly. And they smell funny.

"Window. I want the one by the window," I protest. I don't really care, but I want to rile my brother. There's no reaction. Nuts.

"The man said to go to Orange Mess before we do anything," my mother tells us.

So out we go again. We follow arrows to a building with a sign that reads Orange Mess Hall. It's a huge dining hall. We get in yet-another line, snake our way inside, and pick up a sandwich, an apple, and a glass of powdered milk. Powdered or not, I gulp it down, grit and all.

People mill about. Some eat standing up.

Voices cry out: "Hey, this is crap. I'm trying another mess." "Wait for me." "Move over." "Quit shoving."

I look again for my father. Is he lost? Is he even in the camp?

"Hayaku. Hurry and finish," my mother urges.

Now what? We need to collect bedding before dark—an army-issue blanket and pillow. We claim an extra set for my father.

An old woman watches us warily. "You're lucky," she sighs.

"Lucky?" my mother snaps. Beads of sweat glisten on her forehead.

The woman whispers, "When we got here, we had to stuff bags with straw and sleep on a stable floor."

Disbelief creeps into my mother's voice. "Straw? Stable?"

"I'm not lying," the woman defends herself. "Yes, we're sleeping in horse stables."

"Nani? What?!" my mother exclaims.

"The barracks weren't finished when we came. We even cleaned the stables ourselves," the woman tells us.

Feeling guilty, maybe lucky, or just embarrassed, my mother quickly bows and mumbles, "Excuse us, please."

SHAPES AND SOUNDS AT SANTA ANITA, WATERCOLOR, 22 BY 30 INCHES.
I heard the distinctive sounds of geta, wooden clogs, made by the inmates from scrap wood.

When we reach the barrack, there he is—my father is lying in a heap on a bed.

"Daddy!"

My mother interrupts: "We got our…" but then stops short.

I run to him. "We got your blanket. Where did you get yours?"

He doesn't answer.

My mother turns toward us, ignoring my father. "Put your blankets down and get ready for bed."

I try hard not to cry. "No, Mama, let's go home. We found Daddy, so let's go home. I don't want to camp here."

My mother hands me my pajamas and tells me to change.

I stare at my father curled up on his bed. The morning had begun with such anticipation. He and I were going camping. We were going to have so much fun.

"Wake up, Daddy," I whisper. "Let's go home now."

I get into bed, determined not to cry.

It was a strange night. Searchlights swept our window. Sometimes the light flooded the room, outlining our cots against the slatted walls; then they drained away, leaving ghostly images. Sometimes the light seeped in slowly, probing like a gelatinous creature. Sometimes the streams of light appeared red, resembling blood washing the walls. Light—dark, light—dark, over and over again throughout the night. Footsteps passed by, some marching angrily, some shuffling quietly. Voices from all directions disturbed my sleep. They mumbled. They cried. Babies wailed. Skeletons lay beneath the barrack. A bony hand thrust up a white surrender flag. Pine sap oozed from the fresh-cut lumber, and its sharp tang enveloped me. When I awoke, I found beads of pitch tangled in my hair.

Morning was a confusion of banging doors, bawling babies, shouts in Japanese and English, a search for toothbrushes and towels, and a dash for the bathroom.

My father did not get up.

We tiptoed out.

Clangs and bongs assaulted us. Each mess hall had its own signal; Morse codes rang from all sectors of the camp. Our mess hall was a beehive.

My family (left to right): my father, Kanesaburo; my brother, Sumiya; my mother, Yoshiko; and me around 1937.

My brother wolfed down his oatmeal and ran off to find seconds at another mess hall.

When we returned to our room, my father was gone.

"Where did he go?" I asked, but of course my mother didn't know.

"Probably to eat. He'll come back soon."

Neither statement was true. He didn't return until dark. Almost every day that summer, my father was an elusive shadow.

Once I asked him where he went.

"I don't like it here," he replied, looking at me vacantly; he paused for a second and then repeated, "I don't like it here."

"I don't, either. I hate it," I said, hoping that my agreement would win a tiny bit of reassurance.

My father admiring my new kimono and my brother's cowboy outfit in 1937.

"Life is no fun. This camp is…" His voice trailed off, and he walked away.

My mother clipped, "It's better that he's gone."

Better that he's gone? What did she mean? This man is my father. He belongs with us…here. I felt that he was becoming less a person and more that number—18286—a total stranger. My father's spirit seemed to have vanished.

No, it wasn't just Daddy—all of us were gone. Physically, true, we had left our lives in Los Angeles, but this empty feeling emerged from a space deep inside my body. It welled up, spread like a chill, and infected my entire being. Except there was nothing there. Gone. The word was so empty and final: gone.

SUNDAYS IN HOLLYWOODLAND

The hours became days; the days turned into weeks. I forgot the flutter of hope that I'd felt—thinking of this "camping trip" as the beginning of a new relationship with my father.

Before the war, we had a semblance of some coherence in our family life: shared meals, Buddhist temple services, community picnics. And we

THE TWO OF US, WATERCOLOR, 30 BY 22 INCHES.
My brother and me, holding my teddy bear, in a somber pose.

had lived in Hollywood—a poor section, to be sure, but Hollywood, home of the movie stars. Hollywood meant glamor—all those blonde-haired, red-lipped, leggy women wrapped in furs waving cigarette holders. Our house was within walking distance of Monogram Studios. My friend Aiko and I would stand in front of the locked gates hoping to glimpse a movie star, even one of the cowboys from a sagebrush saga that this studio featured.

If my mother drove us a few miles, we could see the Hollywoodland sign. Below that sign, we knew, glitter, fame, and fun flourished. At night the sign glowed with hundreds of light bulbs, visible for miles. We both vowed to climb to the sign one day. It never happened.

HOME, WATERCOLOR, 30 BY 22 INCHES.
The days after Pearl Harbor were rife with rumors. In the painting,
a soldier's feet bear down on us. My mother and father stoically face the future.

And now it never would. Never. Look at us. We lived in a barrack at a racetrack. Would anything ever be normal again?

One cherished memory: a summer Sunday at the beach. One entire day with my father. We crammed into the car, my aunts Evelyn and Frances and Sumiya in the backseat, and me, wedged between my parents in the front with the gearshift stick butting up against my knees. My mother drove, gripping the knob of the gearshift with her right hand and the steering wheel with her left.

"Move your legs," she ordered.

I tucked my knees under my chin, but they knocked into my face with every rut in the road.

"Here," my father said and moved his legs against the door.

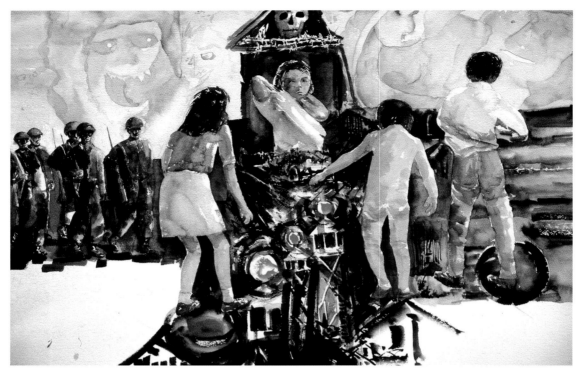

NIGHT STORY, WATERCOLOR, 30 BY 22 INCHES.
My fears multiplied at night. I wondered if I would be killed or sent away to Japan.

I lowered my legs. I felt the muscles in his thigh, warm and knotted. My father edged away, folded his arms across his chest, and stared at the road.

When we crossed the drawbridge, the ocean air beckoned, sharp and salty. As we sped closer, I squirmed out of my dress—I had my bathing suit already on beneath my clothes so I might dash into the waves without wasting a second.

Some concession stands stood guard on the beach pathway. One displayed celluloid Kewpie dolls on sticks. I coveted that chubby-cheeked doll with her twist of hair pointing out the top her head, silver beads around her neck, pink feathers circling her waist. My mother never yielded to my pleas, but maybe my father would buy me one.

"Daddy…" I tried my sad voice.

"What?" He glanced at my mother. *She's your problem,* he seemed to be saying.

"Nothing." I dashed for the foaming edge of the water.

It was a magical afternoon. I chased each wave's sudsy edge as it retreated, and I scurried back into the squishy sand as the water kissed my ankles. My father kicked at the surf. My aunts flung water over me, the droplets glittering like diamonds. Their legs churned the water; their arms spun in circles. In bathing suits, their breasts were molded like plaster, straining against the wet fabric.

I hope I have breasts like that. Soft and round and kind of bouncy. That's what makes women different from men. Men have that thing hanging like a weenie between their legs. "Pee-nee-su," my mother called it. I saw my father's once. He was lying in the bathtub, knees bent, his pee-nee-su floating like a dead fish. He quickly covered it with his washcloth. "Did you cover it because it was cold?" I asked. "Yes," he answered.

Now he plopped down in the sand in his navy blue shorts, and my brother began heaping sand over him. I ran to help. His legs were already covered, but there it was, that bulge. I scooped some sand and dropped it there. My father swatted my hands. "Hey, cut that out!"

I ran away, giggling.

My mother went barefoot but never changed into a bathing suit.

Aunt Frances explained, whispering, "Your mother can't go into the water today because it's 'that time' of the month."

"What about the time?"

"It's something that happens when you grow up."

"What happens?" I asked, but I didn't wait for explanations. I ran off to make castles and watch them melt in the tide. I untangled the seaweed that wrapped around my legs, dragged a piece onto the shore, and decorated my father's chest with the slimy rope. He reached up to feel the squishy pods but left them there. "Thank you," he said, his eyes still closed.

Later, he and I trudged to the roadside stand and—oh, happiness—bought double-scoop cones for everyone.

When the sun finally sat close to the horizon, it was time to head home. We tossed our lunch scraps into a paper sack, whipped the sand from the blanket, and furled the umbrella on its staff. The sun blazed red, painting a

Left to right: Aunt Mitsuko Evelyn, my father, my brother, Aunt Misako Frances, and me at Huntington Beach in July 1937.

tattered ribbon toward the shore, and sank. It left behind a thin purple line on the horizon that disappeared when I blinked.

I fell asleep in the car. In the morning, I felt the residue of sand in my bed and thought about the perfect day at the beach.

Only one day. One perfect day. I envied my brother whom my father obviously favored. They had had so many perfect days...those Sunday fishing trips to Terminal Island and San Pedro, sunrise to sunset. My brother said the two of them mostly sat and waited for the fish to bite, that they didn't talk much. But they both appeared exhilarated when they returned, a string of fish perhaps dangling from their hands.

Then in the summers, my father sometimes let Sumiya accompany him to work in Beverly Hills, where he attended to the estates of William Wyler, Betty Hutton, Jerry Colonna, and Edward G. Robinson—Hollywood big shots. My brother helped mow, rake, and trim. For lunch they patronized a grocery store on Sunset Boulevard, bought cold drinks, and ate their sandwiches in the truck. My father's job appeared so glamorous—rubbing shoulders with celebrities—and Sumiya got to share that excitement.

We were poor, but I didn't know any Japanese families who didn't scrimp and save. However, now, with my father—and later both my father and mother—earning a steady income working for a couple named Harrington three days a week, my mother was able to pursue her dressmaking career, and my father sought other part-time jobs. The Hollywood rich people enjoyed a gardener who could also stir up a quick lunch on demand. Leftovers from these meals occasionally provided us with fruit or vegetables, or, even better, a misshapen éclair. My father began searching for a more reliable truck and told Sumiya and me that we might look at bicycles for Christmas presents.

•

My parents listened to the nightly news and subscribed to the *Los Angeles Times*. On Sunday the announcer described the comic strips. I was annoyed that he told about the action, rather than reading the balloons verbatim. I wanted to follow the script as if it were a play. "That's not what it says here," I complained to my mother, but she was intent on the society and fashion section. She collected pictures of the latest fashions from magazines and newspapers and tidily pasted them into a notebook. "See," she said, "my own *Vogue*. Maybe my customers will like these new styles."

•

We first learned of the "liberation" of Southeast Asia and China from foreign powers by the Japanese when the story hit the front page of the paper. Manchukuo was freed from bondage. The occupation of China in 1937 was declared a Holy War. My uncles suggested that my parents repatriate to Japan, that they might be safer there, but they offered no further explanation. Shortly thereafter my mother's brothers were drafted into the Imperial Army. The military had inspired the country by proclaiming Hakko Ichiu, the doctrine of the Eight Corners of the Earth. England had occupied India and other countries and expanded its empire—Japan would emulate the British. The emperor was descended from the goddess Amaterasu and, thus, was obligated—as a living god of the Land of the Rising Sun—to extend peace and justice throughout the world. However, much of the world,

My father with his employer's dog and automobile in January 1928.

including the United States, viewed Japan's actions as aggression. Roosevelt called Japan a "war machine."

The conflicting views confused my parents, but the daily details of their lives took precedence, and they didn't stop to explore their emotions and positions on the topic. There was little time to ponder the political machinations of the world.

Japan saw itself being strangled and retaliated. The Japanese attacked Pearl Harbor on December 7, 1941.

It was a Sunday. The world reeled. So did we.

ARCADIA, NO. 2

As we settled into our bewildering lives at Santa Anita, clashing mess bells controlled our days. *Clang, clang, ding, ding, bong, ka-ching*—a chorus of rhythms and tones rang out three times a day. In the evenings, we surrendered ourselves to the block captain making bed checks. The first few weeks he knocked, poked his head in, and counted each of us, but later he simply tapped on the door and asked us to verify our number. "Yes, we're here," one of us answered, but sometimes my father was missing. We wouldn't have known what to say if he had looked in and seen only three of us.

WAITING FOR THE ORANGE MESS TO OPEN, WATERCOLOR, 30 BY 22 INCHES.
At Santa Anita, each mess hall had a designated color. Ours was orange.
The lines of people seemed to wander on forever.

Monday was inspection day. We dragged our belongings outside onto the asphalt. Only beds remained inside. Sometimes, though, the police walked in and felt beneath the mattresses. They checked the goods spread on the street and confiscated anything on the contraband list, sometimes more. Radios and cameras were banned outright. A photographer with a studio in Japantown had constructed a camera from found objects and hoped that his Caucasian assistant would bring him some lenses, but his partner had fled with all the equipment. Undaunted, he constructed a simple camera. A friend smuggled in film, then returned to retrieve it and have it developed.

The government banned photos that recorded life within the assembly centers, so the police desperately tried to find the camera before more photographs were taken. Soon they suspected everyone of sneaking in photographic materials. The police rifled through boxes, pillows, suitcases—sometimes even the pockets or clothes we wore.

"Nanda, kore? What is this?" Omi-san toed the pajamas that I had folded into an imaginary sleeping figure, one sleeve tucked under the collar, legs bent at the knees.

"My pajamas, Mr. Omi," I said.

"Don't be smart," he growled.

"What?"

"Do it right."

"I don't know…" I began before I glimpsed my mother's warning look. "Yes, Mr. Omi," I said dutifully. I picked up the pajamas and gathered them into a bundle.

When everything was hauled back into our room, I folded my pajamas on my bed into another figure—arms raised in surrender, legs splayed.

"I give up, Mr. Omi, O-mi-oni, O-mi-oni, Mr. O-mi devil," I chanted and stretched my arms toward the ceiling. "Mom, the white police don't care how sloppy our stuff is. Why do the Japanese police fuss so much?"

"I don't know, but look: this time they took my sewing needles. *Kanten sakana beetsu!*"

"Mama!" My mother seldom used this fractured phrase. I told her we'd find new ones, but I didn't know how. Some lucky people had outside friends bring them supplies—clothes, books, flashlights—but we weren't one of those lucky families. My parents had neither the time nor the know-how to make Caucasian friends. They worked for white people; they didn't socialize with them.

"The police take anything they want," my mother cried as she hit the wall with her fist.

"Do they really sell the stuff on the outside?" I asked.

"Who told you that?"

"Someone at school."

"When Japanese take from other Japanese, something is very wrong. Japanese always support each other. We must stand together."

"That's why people call them *inu*," I said.

"*Baka inu,* stupid spy," my mother emphasized.

The Issei were frugal. They ripped apart rice sacks and sewed them into underwear. They mended and remended sheets until they resembled patchwork. They took apart old dresses and transformed them into children's clothes or pajamas. A few needles could do all of that. My mother told me how her mother had made her count the number of pins and needles before she began a project, then recount them before putting her work away. If a single pin was missing, she had to find it before she could eat or go to bed.

Yes, a needle was a very precious thing, but the police didn't care. They exerted their puffed-up authority by taking needles.

•

A temporary school was organized to make up for three months of lost time. We were scattered in small clusters across the bleachers in the grandstand. The clamor was overwhelming. Most of the time I could barely hear our teacher, Miss Nakasuji.

I shared a single geography text with four other kids. One page featured a photo of Japanese women, their hair swept up in smooth pompadours like huge dinner rolls. They smiled shyly and shaded themselves with parasols.

"This is dumb," I blurted. "No one in Japan wears hairdos like this anymore."

"Never mind. We're not studying Japan," Miss Nakasuji said dismissively.

I slammed the book on the bleacher.

A disembodied male voice crackled through a bullhorn: "Attention, students."

Miss Nakasuji quickly reminded us, "It's time for the pledge. Stand up. Hands over your hearts."

Left hand? No, it was the right. "I pledge allegiance to the flag of the United States of America and to the republic for which it stands…"

Why were we still pledging our allegiance to the United States? The government had classified us as evil Japanese and herded us into this camp. Maybe we ought to be singing the Japanese anthem instead. Kimigayo wa… Yes, I knew that anthem. My mother had taught it to me because, she claimed, "You are Japanese, Yuriko." "Japanese? No, I'm American," I insisted. But I had learned it anyway because it was so beautiful, such a sad melody. I had no idea of its meaning, but I knew the words ishi *and* koke, *rocks and moss. It must have something to do with nature.*

The stadium echoed with a mob of voices. "…and to the republic for which it stands." The words vibrated up and down the bleachers.

Below me a group of high school boys stood with their hands clasped behind their backs. No one else seemed to notice. I had seen these boys before, loitering at the base of the stadium, cigarettes dangling from their lips.

"…with liberty and justice for all."

We sat down. However, the boys below continued to stand. Now other students took notice and watched.

The boys snapped their arms in a mock military salute.

"What are they doing?"

"Show-offs."

"They're gutsy," a student commented, admiration in his voice.

"…part of the Blades."

"Blades?"

"One of the L.A. gangs."

The boys marched away, legs moving in unison. Their teacher did not stop them.

I fought an impulse to escape with them. Just stand and go. How hard was that? Just go. Now. Yet I couldn't force my bottom off the bench.

Flies buzzed around us as if we were a picnic lunch. I swished them away with my arms and legs.

"Quit kicking me!" This came from Tiz, Miss Crybaby.

"I didn't do it on purpose," I protested.

Tiz edged away.

"Yuriko!" Miss Nakasuji snapped.

"Yes?"

"Please sit still!" That same command again.

"OK." I nudged Tiz's foot.

"Teacher, Yuriko's kicking me," she exclaimed.

Miss Nakasuji sighed in exasperation.

I hoped she would tire of my fidgeting and punish me once again by sending me home. I'd rather be there than plastered to this hard bench, reading from a tattered book in the sweltering heat.

Life was made for moving around: running, hopping, playing tag and red rover. Before the war at the annual Japanese School sports' day, I had placed second in a race and won a bronze pendant etched with two racers hand in hand. My mother was at the finish line clapping. She offered me a chain from which I could hang my *takara,* my treasure.

On a blanket under a huge tree, we ate lunch, a Japanese meal packed in *jubako,* lacquered stacking boxes... rice balls, lotus root, fish cakes, sweet lima beans, teriyaki chicken. What a feast. We traded *ânpan* and *mochigashi.* I loved these confections, especially the soft pink *mochi* wrapped in cherry-blossom leaves.

I wanted the day to last forever.

When report cards appeared at the school, I wasn't surprised to see an N ("needs to improve") checked next to "works hard" and "makes good use of time." But why hadn't she marked an N next to "obeys cheerfully"? Teachers were weird.

All day I heard, "Yuriko, please pass this paper."

"Yes, teacher."

"Yuriko, please change seats with Tommy."

"Yes, teacher."

"Yuriko, please stop humming."

"Yes, teacher."

"Yuriko, please pay attention."

"Yes, teacher."

"Yuriko, please stop talking."

"Yes, teacher."

I scowled. Maybe this was Miss Nakasuji's definition of "cheerful." I willed all my wits to keep "No!" bottled inside. *"Gaman,"* I cautioned myself. *"Gaman.* Endure and be patient. Yes, *gaman."*

A parent had to sign the report card. I decided to find my father because he would scan the card, only interested in finding the line to scrawl his signature. He didn't care about my grades. He never asked about school, how I was doing. My mother, however, would mete out her silent treatment.

When I arrived home, Mrs. Satomura was sitting on the steps of the room next door. I asked if she'd seen my father.

"He's inside with my husband but don't disturb them right now."

"Why not?"

"Because I said so. You think you can do anything you want. You're such a spoiled brat."

I felt my face flush. I bolted into our room and flung myself on a cot.

A brat? How dare she! I'd go back and swear at her. I'd stomp my feet and yell: "Dumbbell." *"Baka!"* "Stupid!" "Your boys are lousy brats." I'd give her the finger. Maybe I'd even slap her.

But I didn't do any of those things. A lump lodged in my throat. I gritted my teeth. I didn't want to bawl like a baby, but I did. Not big tears, just those burning "I-hate-you" tears that oozed out despite *gaman.*

Then I heard my father's voice trembling through the wall: "More."

Mr. Satomura replied with a tumble of indistinct words. A long silence followed.

Sometime later I peered outside. Mrs. Satomura was gone. "Dad?" No answer. I nudged open the door. "Daddy? Mr. Satomura?"

My father and Mr. Satomura were both snoring on the same bed. I was struck by the reek of alcohol. My father stirred.

"Daddy, I need you to..."

"Go. Away."

"I need you to sign my report card."

"Not now," he slurred and rolled over on his side.

In the end, it was my mother who signed my card and, as expected, I got the silent treatment. This time it lasted only two days. Not that bad.

●

I thought about my father, his absence, his distancing. He was an apparition that appeared briefly and disappeared over and over from my life. Like my mother, he had grown up in a small rural hamlet tacked onto the fringes of a larger city. Both my parents had ended their formal educations in the sixth grade, but the similarities ended there. My mother had assumed family responsibilities; my father had emigrated to America.

My brother and I called him Daddy. So did my mother, except when she was exasperated or angry at him...then it was "You, *anta*." My aunts called him *neesan,* elder brother. He was Kay, sometimes Ken, to his friends. His real name was Kanesaburo, but no one—not even his parents—used it. They knew him only as the stranger son they had left in Japan as a newborn. His mother was only sixteen and escaped to America with her lover after giving birth. He was raised by his Uncle Chonozo and his family.

"Your daddy didn't like the *inaka,* countryside. He ran away to Wakayama City a couple of times. His uncle found him the first time, and they made him watch the family eat but wouldn't feed him. He didn't tell me much more. I think it was too painful. Poor Daddy," my mother told me.

I imagined this little boy—perhaps nine or ten—sometimes hitching wagon rides but mostly walking toward Wakayama and resting, tucked against trees and fences. How far twenty miles must have seemed. How happy he must have been to reach the Pacific Ocean and then wonder how he could cross that vast expanse to a place called Ka-ri-fo-ni-ya and find his parents. His uncle assured him that his parents would send for him one day.

On his second attempt, he actually found a job for a month as an errand boy at a small family restaurant and lived in a tiny space in the back between sacks of rice. Before dawn he accompanied the owner to the fish market and learned how to choose the best of the catch..."alert" eyes, shiny skin, fresh ocean smell. And the shape, yes, the shape had to be perfect. If the fish

My father's family (left to right): his mother, Kofusa Nakai; my father, Kanesaburo; his baby sister, Misako Frances; and his father, Kusuemon Nakai, in 1913.

were deformed in some minute way—missing scales, having a clipped fin, or being a strange color—these were *obake,* hobgoblins, and would bring bad luck to the restaurant. My father learned how to brew fine green tea: the water was boiled to the tiny-bubble stage. He heard the water sing in the

Chonozo Nakai, my father's uncle, and my father on the eve of his departure for America in 1912. His uncle had raised him.

iron kettle before the bubbles burst. If he was only a few seconds early or late, the tea would not "accept" the water. He learned to prepare vegetables for pickling, pressing down the slices in brine with wood and stones.

He was so happy. The owner told my father that as he learned the trade, he would pay him a few coins. But one day there *he* was...his uncle stood over him as he straddled the hole in the backyard. My father quickly pulled up his pants and, without a word, his uncle led him inside to gather his meager belongings, and they trudged home in the gathering dark. This time, however, they shared the rice balls and pickles that the owner had hastily packed for them.

When he was twelve, my grandmother, Fusa Nakai, returned to Japan to escort my father to California. He attended public school, but there were no provisions for immigrant students, and he found himself herded into a second-grade class. Humiliated, he quit on the spot. He must have had a flair for calligraphy or art, however, because the few letters I remember my mother receiving from him were written in English with great flourishes.

His life, however, was bereft of ornaments. He struggled with job after job. Remembering his aborted, but happy, experience in the restaurant, he opened a small café in Los Angeles, but, because he had no business expertise, it floundered. He discovered that alcohol could erase his frustrations, and, once hooked, he could not climb out of the deep abyss it created.

"Poor Daddy," I agreed with my mother. And so it was that we both accepted this man who came and went, ghostlike, in our lives.

•

One afternoon in July some mess bells began to sound in the middle of the afternoon. I ran home to find my mother standing immobile outside our barrack door. She grabbed my arm and pushed me into our room.

"What's wrong? What's happening?!" I cried.

More mess bells clanged in confusion. The distant wail of a siren moaned through the din.

"What's going on?"

"I don't know. Mrs. Satomura said some troublemakers are rioting. They make trouble for all of us."

"What do you mean?"

"We come to camp. No trouble. We do like the government wants. No trouble. If we *gaman*. If we endure…there's no trouble, but some people are troublemakers."

"I want to go see."

"We need to stay inside. Be safe. Be safe."

"Everyone's out there."

"I will take care of you. Nothing bad will happen to you."

"I can't do anything exciting just because I'm a girl."

"In Japan girls don't look for excitement. They take care of the family."

"Mama, this isn't Japan. It's America."

"America," my mother murmured and looked out the window as if "America the Beautiful" were a picture hanging outside the camp.

"This is America," she repeated.

Then, to my astonishment, my mother began to cry: softly, quietly, at first…then a keening, heaving wail. She sank onto her bed.

I didn't know what to do. This was my mother. This was the woman who was always strong. She knew what to do, how to handle everything. She was the one who carried on whenever my father disappeared. Now I heard the cry of a lost child, a soul wandering down some meandering path with no light at the end.

"Mama? Don't cry," I whispered, but she didn't hear me. Her sorrow was overwhelming. She sobbed until her tears were used up. She groped for me, and I sat down by her side. She reached for my hand. She gripped it so hard it hurt.

"You know," she whispered.

"What?"

"Maybe I would do the same thing."

"What do you mean?" I was scared. I had never heard anyone cry like this before.

"I would be a troublemaker."

"You?"

"I made trouble for my father in Japan."

SHIKATAGANAI

When my mother was four or five, my grandfather, a Buddhist priest, tied her to a tree in back of the temple because she was disobedient. She was tired and hungry; her mother had gone somewhere with her infant son, and my mother had asked for food, but her father, determined to finish writing his sermon, ignored her. So she toddled down the embankment to a neighbor's house and asked for a snack, a rice ball, perhaps. The neighbor fed her. My mother asked for a second helping. The woman, furious at my mother's bad manners, grabbed her and half dragged her up to the temple.

She described the situation to my grandfather, who, humiliated, apologized for my mother's rude behavior.

"For shame! *Mittomo nai koto!*" my grandfather scolded.

In the yet-stratified society of late-Meiji Japan, especially in the rural areas, people were expected to adhere to established codes of behavior, and my mother had broken one. A person on a higher social level never asked a favor of someone of lesser rank, except in dire or sinister circumstances. Although my mother's family was poor and lived as the entire village did—from hand to mouth—my grandfather was a priest. His status was high, and therefore it was he who ministered to his parishioners, not the other way around. He admonished my mother and told her to wait quietly on the veranda while he composed his sermon.

My mother sat and gazed at the bamboo plants. She had been told that if you waited and watched, you could see the bamboo grow, hear it mew softly like a kitten. She wondered why it was so bad to ask for something to eat when your stomach was growling from hunger. She sat and wondered and stared at the bamboo. The bamboo didn't grow. It didn't make a sound. Her stomach felt as if a hand were squeezing it. She felt nauseous. She knew she was going to throw up.

She ran to her father. When my mother interrupted him a second time, he lost his patience, hauled her to a pine tree, and tied her there. My mother began to bawl, crying out, over and over, "I'm sorry. Let me go. I'm sorry." She cried for a long time. Finally, the neighbor, feeling contrite, untied the ropes and took my mother home with her. Shortly after, my grandmother returned, retrieved my mother, and fed the family dinner.

My mother finished her story. "Patience is good," she said, "but only when your stomach is full."

I tried to console her: "You were only a baby. It wasn't your fault."

"I didn't obey, and a bad thing happened."

I squeezed her hand tighter, even though it made the pain worse.

We sat like that for a long time. Then the mess bells began to ring again, but this time in coordinated rhythm.

Dinner talk buzzed about the afternoon disturbance. Hot plates used in the barracks to heat milk for babies had triggered the riot. Outsiders had smuggled in these appliances to desperate mothers. The electrical system had overloaded and blown the grid. Fuses were impossible to buy. Pennies placed in the fuse box caused minor fire damage. The police were ordered to confiscate the offending hot plates, but rumor spread that they were stealing other items, including money. Some said they had torn up mattresses and pillows. Some even claimed they had tried to rape a young woman. Mayhem erupted, but the protesters were outnumbered by armed police. The riot leaders were jailed and, with other problem dissenters, sent to Tule Lake or Manzanar, the most closely guarded camps.

The next day was extraordinary because it was so ordinary. After the disturbance, I had expected to awaken into a different world. But the barracks looked the same, and I ate at the Orange Mess and came home to a room with four beds. The protest had made no difference.

•

Soon after the riot, some older boys began taunting the soldiers in the towers. They dared each other to touch the barbed wire circling the camp, knowing that it would alert the guards.

"Double dare, double dare," they whispered.

One boy stepped toward the fence.

"Cluck, cluck, chicken," the bystanders taunted, flapping their elbows and mocking the boy.

From the safety of a barrack wall, I watched these ducktailed young toughs in pegged pants.

"You and Sumiya stay away from those boys," my mother had ordered. *"Yogores,"* she called them in a disapproving tone. "They are trash." However, these boys were considered "smooth" by high-school girls, who blushed whenever one of them leered or whistled.

Now, however, doubt replaced the bravado in the expression of the boy approaching the fence.

"Halt!" the soldier called out, but he, too, sounded uncertain.

The other boys silently flapped their elbows a bit more tentatively.

The boy being egged on took a tiny step.

The soldier struck his rifle against the wall.

My heart pounded. "Soldiers shoot to kill," I had heard.

Around the corner and one barrack away, people were laughing and chattering. Hadn't they heard the soldier hit his rifle against the tower? Couldn't they sense the danger? Their laughter seemed surreal.

The boy took another step.

"Do it, do it, do it," the boys chanted softly. "Do it, do it, do it."

"Halt!" The soldier raised his rifle and took aim.

I could hardly breathe. Everything froze.

Suddenly, I heard a footstep and turned to see Mrs. Satomura walking up behind me. She glanced at the boys and chastised them: "Hey, boys, you doing a stupid thing."

"Shh…" I cautioned.

Too late. The boys turned and scowled. "You dumb broad, whadaya doing?"

"Just watching," I mumbled.

"You wrecked everything."

I turned to Mrs. Satomura. "Why are you here?"

"Your mother wants you."

"Yeah, go home, dumb chick," one boy sneered.

The boy close to the fence retreated.

"Chicken," another boy scoffed at him.

"Naw, wasn't no good." The retreating boy looked straight at me and said, "I coulda done it."

"Oh, yeah? Double dare," the others retorted.

"No, I gotta go." The boy sauntered away with an exaggerated swagger.

"Yeah, chicken," the other boys hooted.

The boy walked on without a backward glance.

So did I.

•

Laundry day was a clamorous adventure. We scrubbed clothes in round metal tubs on washboards. If we were early, we were rewarded with warm water. If we were late, the water was cold. The soap, a harsh-smelling brown block, left a peculiar odor that lingered for days on our hands and the clothes. Sometimes bits of lint and soap chips stuck to the clothes. If they itched, I rinsed them again in the bathroom.

A few fortunate women used Lux flakes or Oxydol soap, but they never shared. No one complained. Most women relished laundry time as a chance to gossip and catch up on the latest rumors.

"Relocation to the permanent camps has started."

"Already?"

"I heard that people in the stables go first."

"To Heart Mountain?"

"They're going to Arkansas."

"You can bribe some authorities to be sent to Poston, Arizona. I hear the weather's sunny like California."

"I just want to go home."

Basha, basha.

"We got a day pass to check our house. Our neighbors are looking after it."

"How is it on the outside?"

"Scary. People wouldn't talk to us. One man yelled at us to get off the bus. Complained to the driver that we were Jap spies."

"What'd the driver do?"

"Nothing, but he kept glancing at us in the mirror. Maybe he thought we were going to blow up the bus."

Basha, basha.

"The Okimotos' house was ransacked. They asked the police to investigate, but the police didn't do anything."

"Nothing they can do. *Shikataganai.*"

"What do you mean, 'can't be helped'? The police are probably the ones who took everything."

"You're right. They know which houses are empty."

"Shikataganai."

"There you go again…can't be helped. You give up too easily."

"If we do what the government wants, they'll let us go home sooner."

"If there's any place to go home to."

Basha, basha.

"I heard that woman is making a lot of money."

"The Black Spider?"

I lifted my hands out of the suds and wiped them on my apron. "Why is she called that?"

"She walks around in a black slip."

My mother glared at the woman who had answered.

Basha, basha.

"Did the police really kill a man yesterday?"

"They'll shoot at anything."

"They're target-practicing."

"I hear the white guys are visiting the Spider. Giving her stockings."

My mother turned to me. "Yuriko, this talk is for big people. Take the clothes and hang them up."

I took my time. I wanted to hear grown-up talk. Nevertheless, I did as I was told, and when my mother returned to our room, I asked, "Did the guard really kill someone?"

"Only a rumor. Don't worry."

"When I was watching those guys by the fence, the guard looked ready to shoot."

"Just pretending."

"You sent Mrs. Satomura to get me."

"It was getting late. I didn't want you to miss dinner."

"How did you know where I was?"

"I knew."

"Mama, I'm scared. Maybe they're not pretending."

"Nothing to worry about."

I didn't believe her.

●

One night I awoke with an urgent need to use the bathroom. The toilets were four barracks away. I peered out the window. A door banged. A dog barked. A dog? Pets weren't allowed. It began to howl. A man called out…then silence. A child cried out, "Mama! Mama!" Footsteps passed beneath my window. Maybe if I concentrated—thought about something else—I wouldn't have to go. Was the soldier in his tower moving the searchlight all night long? Was he alone? No use—I had to get to the toilet.

I felt for my shoes, slipped them on, and padded outside. It was only a few steps to the corner of our barrack. Then, wham! A brilliant light slammed into me. For a second, I didn't know what it was. It felt like a physical blow. I whirled around and started back to our room. No, I couldn't go back; I'd wet my pants. My heart pounded. The spotlight seared my face. Step by step. Another step. When I finally reached the bathroom, I was trembling. I pressed against the door. *Calm down. He won't shoot.*

Even in my hurry, I remembered my mother's warning: "Dirty germs on toilets. You can get something and die." I swiped the seat with paper and laid down some sheets before sitting down. I sat a long time, hoping that the soldier would forget about me. Naked toilet bowls squatted in a row like upside-down plungers ready to suck all the darkness into the sewers. A faucet dripped into a metal sink with a hollow echo. A cockroach scuttled across the floor.

How to get back? Wait until the light raked past, then dash out and stay close to the barracks? If I screamed, would someone rescue me? I took a deep breath and opened my mouth to make a sound, but nothing came out. Just a weak "aahhh."

I had to go back. I cracked open the door. The light swept by. Could I sneak along and sidestep against the barracks? I recalled my mother's remark that she could be a troublemaker. Well, I wasn't making trouble now.

THE LIGHTS SEARCHING, WATERCOLOR, 22 BY 30 INCHES.
One night on my way to the bathroom several buildings away, a guard trained his searchlight
on me. I thought he might kill me. Years later, my husband commented that the guard
could have been helpfully lighting my way.

I hadn't done anything wrong. The guard had no reason to shoot. My heart was pounding. I was scared, but I also resented the guard and the intrusion of the light.

I flung open the door and strode into the center of the beam. *Walk normally. Don't look scared.* The guard trained the light on me. I walked back—step by anxious step—down the middle of the road. It was so far. Four barracks felt like a mile. As soon as I reached my barrack, the spotlight swept past me and out into the hollow black.

I was still alive.

I climbed into bed. Had it been real? Had I been dreaming? No, the searchlight still blinked across the window…over and over. I closed my eyes. The rhythm flickered against my eyelids…light, dark, light, dark. The beat went on and on.

When I fell asleep, I dreamed about hovering above an ocean. Skeletal fish lay inert, then thrashed about as predators nibbled away at them. A soldier shot at the fish with a popgun. I dropped into the water and sank slowly into its layers: clear—muddy, clear—muddy. I rocked as if I were in a cradle.

GASA GASA BABY TELLS ALL

Some years before we arrived at camp, my mother returned home with a small doll from Mrs. Harrington. I loved this blonde-haired doll with her blue eyes, slender legs, and gentle bumps for breasts. After school my friend Aiko brought her doll, and we played house on the back porch. Usually Aiko tired of the game sooner than I did and went home, but I continued to pretend, constructing scenarios and conversations between my doll and her imaginary friends. One day I gathered some yellow yarn, made a hula skirt, and circled her neck with a lei of pink tissue paper. The doll was hinged at the waist, so I rotated her hips to make her dance. Looping rubber bands across a box, I fashioned a ukulele and sang to my wahine.

I wished I had my doll with me at Santa Anita. There had been a talent show. In one routine, two women had done the hula in bright red glittery skirts. My doll would have been beautiful in such a skirt. The yarn one now seemed drab in my memory, like everything here—gray and tan and black.

"Mama, what happened to my doll?" I asked her.

"There was no room for toys. The government allowed only one suitcase for each of us."

"Why didn't you ask me?"

"When the government ordered us to move, I did everything myself," my mother snapped. "No one helped. You and Sumiya were at school. Daddy was working. We only had ten days' notice. I couldn't pack everything that everyone wanted."

"She was so special. I loved her. Where is she now?"

"I don't know."

"Mama, can I get a hula skirt?"

The astonished look on her face was my answer.

"I want to hula."

"That's a bad dance."

"Why?"

"Only bad women move their hips like that. I raised you to be a good girl when you grow up."

"It's only a dance, Mama." However, I knew there was something risqué about it when the men whistled and cheered "hubba, hubba" as the women gyrated their hips. The cellophane skirts shimmered and rippled like ocean waves. The strands flipped and winked as the women twisted. I was transfixed. I hadn't even minded standing, packed like a sardine on the tarmac.

"No. Don't ask again. No hula skirt," my mother repeated.

"You didn't pack my doll or my teddy bear, either." I pouted.

"After the war is over, I'll buy you another one."

"It's not the same."

"Yuriko, nothing is ever the same. Especially now every day will bring a change. Maybe some will be good. Don't *monku*. Don't complain."

She was right. In a matter of a few weeks, our lives had changed drastically. They no longer included dolls, teddy bears, and homemade hula skirts. Everything had disappeared: my father's broken-down truck, his big

I am hugging a doll given to me by Mrs. Harrington in 1940.

game-fish tails on the garage wall, my brother's secondhand bicycle, my mother's sewing machine, her garden.

My mother usually wore practical, flat-heeled shoes with silk stockings rolled down around her ankles like a donut or some somber-colored anklets. Sometimes, though, when she was gardening, she'd peel off her socks and shoes, place them carefully aside, and step into the dirt.

"Ahh. This feels so good," she always said, squeezing clods with her toes.

Then, embarrassed, she commented on her feet. "I have stubby toes. Farmers' feet. You do, too. So we should never go barefoot in front of other people."

Our California garden was a fair-sized city plot between our house and the street on a gently rounded hillock, and I suppose people on the sidewalk could see her carefully hoeing straight furrows for her seeds, but I doubted

My mother and I holding hands in front of the avocado tree in our front yard in Los Angeles. This is a favorite photograph of mine taken before the war.

they could see her feet, nor did I care if they could. However, it was easier to agree than to discuss farmers' feet.

"OK," I said.

In the spring, my mother's tender care produced crisp peas and lettuce and green onions. Fragile tendrils curled themselves around the twine she had strung between wooden poles, and we plucked a few pods, ate a few, and then picked enough for dinner. I threw the mounds of shells into a compost pile by the incinerator. I hated picking lettuce leaves because a tiny worm might ooze itself onto my fingers. It was slimy and gave me shivers, and I squealed as I flung it away.

"Worms are good, Yuriko. Don't throw it. Put it carefully back into the ground," my mother cautioned.

"OK," I said and ran to the faucet to wash my hands.

As the weather warmed, carrots and beets and summer squash flourished…orange, red, yellow, green. Once in a great while, we had a small watermelon, but for some reason, most turned yellow and soft before they ripened. My mother said it was because her karma was wrong.

And we picked avocados from a tree with glistening leaves. It demarcated the edge of the garden, and it was here in front of this tree that my father, at the insistence of my mother, snapped a photograph of the two of us. We're holding hands, and we both have grins on our faces. It must be Sunday because I am wearing my white Sunday shoes and my putty-colored dress with a swingy full skirt. I used to swirl round and round just to see the fabric ripple in sinuous rhythms.

There were no avocado trees in Santa Anita. More painful, though, than the loss of places and material things I'd once known was the disintegration of our family unit. Granted, we were not the happy movie version of a family, but there had always been the sense of home, a base that grounded our lives. Now we ate our meals, brushed our teeth, and showered with strangers. Now I watched my father retreat further into himself, unable to communicate his feelings. What fragile moments of understanding remained between my parents were fractured beyond repair.

The Japanese—those other war-mongering Japanese—had deprived me of those things. However, I sensed that they were not wholly to blame, that somehow our American government, my government, was also responsible. It had made the decision to rip thousands of people from their homes and place them in isolated camps.

I knew my mother meant more than toys when she had said, "Nothing is ever the same." She had told me how radically her life was altered by her arrival in Seattle in 1923. She had expected her new husband to meet her. Instead, he had appeared a day later with no explanation and told her to throw away the kimono she wore—she must dress Western—she was in America.

CAMOUFLAGING, WATERCOLOR, 22 BY 30 INCHES.
At Santa Anita, the older girls and women created camouflage nets for the U.S. Army.
Today this activity seems ironic—these women were making protective nets for men who were killing
our relatives in Japan while some American soldiers were pointing rifles at us.

Now once more she was uprooted. This new life was even starker than a day's abandonment on a pier. My brother and I were still children, and until we could fend for ourselves, she must carry all the responsibility alone. No, life would never be the same for any of us.

•

Glutted with idle time, young women in the camp responded eagerly to the government's request for workers to construct camouflage nets for the U.S. Army. Hanging at the lower end of the grandstand were huge looms. The women stood on the blacktop, weaving long burlap strips into these dangling nets. The odor of the burlap mixing with the smell of the softened blacktop reminded me of the La Brea Tar Pits. Dinosaurs had met their fate in the oozing tar, bubbling and bursting with a plop. Inside a nearby building were murals of huge reptiles sinking into the muck, roaring and helpless. How did that feel—to be trapped, pulled down by an unknown force? Did the dinosaurs boil to death before being engulfed by the black ooze? Did they know what was happening? Sumiya told me that dinosaurs were cold-blooded so they couldn't feel pain. Was that true? I hoped so. I really hoped so.

My mind drifted back to the women and the nets. The panels were about twelve feet high and just as wide. I didn't see any ladders.

"How do you get the strips into the top part?" I asked.

"Magic."

"No, really."

"Stop bothering us. We've got work to do."

"I'm serious. I really want to know."

The women rolled their eyes and giggled. They ignored me and concentrated on their work.

I returned often to watch their progress. I approached the display imagining a mermaid rising from the ocean and folding herself into one of those seaweedy drapes. Some tiny fish might also be caught, wriggling to get free. She would fling her sleek black hair in an arc, spraying salt water over the

PERSISTENT THREATS, WATERCOLOR, 22 BY 30 INCHES.
The odor of the burlap in the camouflage nets and the softening tar and asphalt of the streets evoked memories of the La Brea Tar Pits in Los Angeles. These pits proved fatal to animals and, I assume, human beings unfortunate enough to become trapped in them.

women. They would look up and laugh, wondering if it were raining. Some of the fish would loosen and glitter like silver droplets in the sea. As I got closer, those undulating pieces of fabric seemed alive. They stirred, crawling like huge eels—trapped, moving. Never still. Like me, just like me.

Once I asked, "Can I help?"

They laughed good-naturedly. "No, you're too young. You have to be older."

"How much older?"

"Not until you have your, you know…"

"What?"

"You'll know soon enough."

"Know what?"

"Go home and ask your mother."

"What about?" No one answered.

It was two years more before I found out.

The irony of this scene dawned on me years later. At Santa Anita, I was bewitched by these nets and saw only gorgeous colors and shapes. In reality these women were creating disguises of green and brown for men who were sent to destroy my relatives.

•

In the summer of 1942, everything ended, and nothing seemed to begin. It was endless. August was scorching. The sun blazed off the asphalt and roasted the elevated barracks. Inside them felt like a baking oven.

One afternoon while I was walking with some friends, we heard a shrill cry from inside a barrack. We peeked in. A baby lay alone on a cot with only a diaper atop its belly.

"It's boiling in here. Why is the baby alone?" someone asked.

"Maybe we ought to take it outside."

"Is it a girl or a boy?" I asked.

"Take a look."

"No, I don't want to."

"Are you scared?"

"You do it if you want to."

"I asked you first."

Finally, I pulled the cloth away. His penis stood upright. Fascinated, we stared at this quivering little peanut.

"My brother said that you make babies with that," I announced.

"With that? How can that be?" one of my friends asked.

"I don't know. But he wouldn't lie."

"It's the mommy who makes babies," someone else said. "I know where people do that."

"Where?"

"On the very top of the stadium at night. People are kissing up there. Wanna check it out?"

The baby began to wail. Just then his mother rushed in, grabbed her baby, and pushed us outside, yelling, "What are you doing?! You're evil! God will punish you!"

I stumbled and scraped my knee on the asphalt.

"You're bad!" she continued to scream.

I cowered in a toilet stall, dabbing away blood with toilet paper. When I returned to our barrack, my mother handed me a gauze bandage.

"Thanks," I said. "Where did that come from?"

"Mrs. Goto gave it to me."

"Who's that?"

"The lady at the end of the barrack. She said you fell down."

"Is she the one with the baby?"

"Yes. Go thank her."

I walked out but ran in the opposite direction from Mrs. Goto's room. My mother had some strange ideas, and this was undoubtedly one of them. Didn't she see who Mrs. Goto was? Someone who abandoned her baby. And what about Mrs. Satomura? My mother liked to gossip with her—a little too much, it seemed to me. Although my parents had had friends to our house in Los Angeles, and I had fallen asleep to their muffled speech and laughter, I had never witnessed an extended one-on-one exchange between my mother and another person. What was Mrs. Satomura's attraction? She was a "glamor girl"—her lips bright red, her eyes black rimmed, her nails long and polished, her hair permed. Perhaps she represented some ideal, a yearning made manifest, a forbidden pleasure.

One evening my mother was perched on one of the steps outside our barrack. I sat down beside her and asked what she and Mrs. Satomura chatted about.

"Just talk."

"She's so different from you."

"We are all Japanese here. Everybody's the same."

"What I mean is she's a lot younger and wears all that makeup."

"Toshi is beautiful inside and out. Don't judge her only from the outside. She tells me about her life before the war. She had a big house with furniture from Japan. She and her husband owned a grocery store. She had a good life. Not like my hard life. She is a Nisei, so she could buy a house. We rented, so I have no house to miss."

"Let's go back and buy one," I suggested

"No, Daddy and I can't because we are Issei. Besides, we are too poor. Dressmaking and gardening are no way to make money. We struggle day to day. I don't want that kind of life for you and Sumiya. I want so much for you to have a better life. It's important to learn English. Then you can find a good job. I can't speak good English, but Toshi can."

"You told me you took English classes."

"Daddy thought it was a waste of time. He didn't want me to go, so I went in secret. After he went to work and Sumiya was in school, I took the streetcar with you and went downtown to a class for Japanese people to learn English."

"I went with you?" I asked.

"At first they let me take you to class. You drew and played with blocks, but it was too long a time for you. You were always a *gasa gasa* baby. You could never sit still. So I took you to the Maryknoll nursery school nearby. The first time you cried so hard that I cried, too. But I had no choice. It was the only thing I could do. I wanted to learn English so badly. The class was only a half day, so I thought it was all right. For one week, I left you there.

On Friday the nun said you should not come back, that you were unhappy there, too."

"A nun? Don't nuns wear long black skirts and a cross?"

"I don't remember a cross."

"She's the one, Mom!" I leaped up. "She's the one who sang the Jesus song. She's the one who hit my hand with a stick."

"She hit…you?" My mother's voice trailed away.

"She was mean."

"I didn't know."

"I didn't make her up! She was real."

"Only for one week. I'm so sorry she hurt you."

"That's OK. It was a long time ago.

"I didn't know what else to do."

"I forgot about her until I saw the woman in that black robe at the church when I was waiting for you."

"I'm sorry."

"You don't need to apologize. You had to do it."

"I'm sorry."

"What about the class? Did you quit?"

"No, no. I made up my mind to learn English. I asked Aunt Frances and Aunt Evelyn to help, and they did but not for long. One time you cried and cried for me—you ran into the middle of the street and cried and didn't stop, so Frances came to get me. You stopped crying as soon as you saw me. They told me you were spoiled and too hard to watch. So I asked *bahchan,* your grandmother, even though I knew she didn't like children. She had a hard time with you, so she told Daddy what I was doing."

"Was he mad?"

"He burned my lessons in the backyard."

"Wow."

"He said women didn't need to learn because they are good for nothing. He said that the education he had was enough, that he could learn what he needed by himself, and so could I."

"So you quit?"

"I had already paid for the lessons, so I went. After that Daddy didn't come home sometimes. He was so angry with me."

"Where did he go?"

"I don't know."

"Just like now. He's never here. Is he mad at us?"

"He's mad at everyone, everything."

"He drinks, too. He and Mr. Satomura were drunk one day."

"Daddy has…um…a problem. I don't know how to help. I don't know what to do."

We were both silent for a while. Then my mother sighed and looked away. "I want you to promise something. Go to college. I will work and pay for you and Sumiya to go to college. After the war, I will work hard. No matter what Daddy says, you go to college."

I was only in the fourth grade and had not given a second's thought to high school, much less to college, but I knew what I needed to say: "Sure, OK. I promise."

"If we were better educated, we would not be here."

"Here?"

"In camp."

"You said Mrs. Satomura is smart, and she speaks good English, but she's here."

My mother drew in her breath as if readying herself for a performance. Then in a torrent of Japanese words, she blurted, "I mean all of Japanese society—Issei, Nisei, Kibei, everyone. We know—everyone knows—it is morally wrong to herd us into camps, but we're unable to stop this terrible reaction. Some people think it was politically motivated. If we were lawyers and teachers and had a command of the laws and the Constitution, maybe we would have known how to defend ourselves and stop the government from executing a mass evacuation of thousands of people. You're an American citizen, Yuriko, and I'm not, but we're both here. We are too scared. 'Yellow bellies,' some people call us. Maybe they're right. We know how to follow. It's the only thing we do well—to follow. When you go to college, you must study two times harder than white people because you are Japanese and can learn well, learn everything. No, maybe three times harder."

I didn't understand some of the Japanese words she used, but I understood the gist of her speech. "Yeah, as if Hakujin will like us better if we're smarter than they are," I replied.

"Americans think we are bad people because we bombed Pearl Harbor."

"I didn't bomb Pearl Harbor. What do you mean 'we'?"

"Japanese people."

"Even you said it. I'm American, Mama, not Japanese. Those Japanese are different from us."

"American citizen, Yuri, American citizen. In spirit we are Japanese. The military in Japan forced the emperor into war. War is a terrible experience. The military warmongers are bad, not the people, not the emperor."

"We used to have a picture of the emperor and empress on the living room wall...what happened to it?" I asked her.

"I burned it. I cried and asked his forgiveness, then I burned it. I knew the government would call us enemies of America and punish us if we kept pictures like that." My mother's voice cracked. "Hirohito is like a God to the Japanese."

She paused. Then gathering composure, she said resolutely, "Let's not talk about this anymore. We are all the same. We are all Japanese. When you are older, you will understand. Yes, you will understand."

2

Settling at Amache

Gaman

I finally got my train ride. This time I had no illusions about what kind of camp awaited me: the permanent one. And we were not campers headed for summer vacation in the woods; we were prisoners.

•

A tired old train hauled us to Amache.

"*Oroshite,* pull down," my mother whispered.

"I want it up." I tugged at the shade. Dust puffed into the air.

"No, down. One of the rules," my mother repeated in Japanese.

"That's dumb."

"No *monku*. Don't complain. Everyone is in the same boat."

"I want to see where we're going."

"Nothing to see."

"Mind your mother," my father clipped.

My mother flinched, momentarily toppled from her perch as disciplinarian. I was jolted by my father's unaccustomed assertiveness. My mother furtively glared at him, refusing to acknowledge his support. My father said no more and stared at the floor. With his hat still on his head, he slumped in a seat across the aisle beside my brother. His cardboard suitcase, trapped in the metal bin above him, threatened to loosen itself onto his head. After

BLESSINGS, WATERCOLOR, 22 BY 30 INCHES.
A Japanese angel is blessing a woman who is praying for the safety of the evacuees.

GOING CAMPING, WATERCOLOR, 30 BY 22 INCHES.
Two children have been told they are going camping, but they are completely unaware of the sort of camp that awaits them.

we had settled into our room at Santa Anita, this suitcase had appeared and disappeared. I had watched my father tuck it under his bed and then retrieve it on several occasions. At the time, the action was not unusual; we all stored items in our suitcases. On two occasions, however, I had peeked under his bed and was surprised to find the space empty. Had he left on a trip? No...impossible. He was imprisoned as we all were. The disappearing suitcase seemed so surreptitious that I didn't dare ask about it.

The train clattered on. I held a diary on my lap. On our final day in Santa Anita, my teacher, Miss Nakasuji, had appeared, handed this diary to me, and said, "This will keep you quiet for a few minutes a day. Stay well."

Confused, I grasped the book. I knew my mother kept a diary, but I had never had one. My teacher said nothing more and walked away. Was this a

TARGET POINT GREEN, WATERCOLOR, 22 BY 30 INCHES.
The location of the Amache Relocation Center was targeted in green in a government publication.
In my painting, a young girl in a colorful kimono is innocently smiling, not realizing her fate.

peace offering? Miss Nakasuji and I were always at odds. She hoped for a quiet and dutiful student. I was neither. She urged me to study harder. I did not. "You have potential." "Stop wasting time." "Stop chattering." "Quit fidgeting." "Write carefully." I hated her imperative comments.

The train stopped at every town on its route and even more often in the middle of nowhere. We chugged along for an hour or two, then shuddered to a stop. Start...stop. Start...stop. Again and again. I lifted the shade high enough to read the station signs and noted them in the diary. Sometimes people on the platform stared incomprehensibly at the train's dark windows. Once a woman waved and smiled. I flipped the shade back into place, afraid I would be identified.

I scribbled my first diary entry: "Stopped at San Bernardino, Barstow. Everyone coughing and sneezing. Hot. Can't open windows. No lunch." I commented about my parents and my brother, about the people and the crummy train. My diary was a sanctuary in this scary place.

Slivers of coal dust filtered in through invisible cracks and speckled our faces. My mother wiped her face.

"You missed," I told her. Mimicking her, I spit on the edge of her handkerchief and touched a spot on her cheek. The cloth was smudged beige and gray with makeup and soot. I felt inexplicably sad. My mother had stitched this handkerchief and delicately embroidered it...not to use herself but to sell door-to-door. Now it had become a washcloth.

"I'm tired," my mother said and closed her eyes. I stared at her.

Did Mom and Dad ever speak with one another? I mean, really talk—those deep serious adult conversations full of frowns and gestures? I wish he were seated next to her now, offering his shoulder to rest her head. In the tiny house in Los Angeles on that futon in the sewing room...did they hold each other? Did they kiss? Aiko said that when a husband and wife kissed, the wife got pregnant. So my mother and father must have kissed each other at least twice, once for my brother and once for me. No, that's not right. I've seen people kissing, and not everyone gets pregnant.

Before the war—after my father left for work—my mother rolled the futon and snuggled it under the plywood table where she cut fabrics and designed dress patterns. I helped her, grunting, *"Yoisho, yoisho,"* to make us laugh. It was funny—the two of us on our knees awkwardly pushing this bulky mat into place.

A dressing table with a large oval mirror squatted in this room. Sitting on a *zabuton,* I brushed my mother's hair. She enjoyed the pampering. She unpinned her long black hair, shook it out, and handed me her brush. I lined up the crimped, U-shaped pins on the table, carefully counting them so we would have the same number, usually ten, when she needed them for the neat bun at the nape of her neck.

One morning my mother told me the story of her mother's unusual hair. "My mother had curly hair so people laughed at her," she said. "Every morning I rubbed my mother's hair with oil to make it straight. Rub, rub, rub. Comb, comb, comb. I complained, but I did it until she told me to stop."

"I wish I had curly hair," I sighed.

"People will call you African. They told my mother to go back to Africa."

"That's mean."

"Japanese are afraid of people who look different. No, not only the Japanese. Americans are the same way."

Now my mother sat exhausted on a rattletrap train, her head jogging up and down as she clutched her handbag on her lap. My brother, too, had fallen asleep, his knees folded on the seat, his stockinged feet draped over my father's lap. My father's hand was curled on my brother's toes. I felt a pang of jealousy. This simple grip seemed such a tender gesture of love and protection, an unconscious display of feeling my father never displayed toward me.

I took out my sketch pad. I drew faces—some with big eyes, some with slits. I remembered that sometimes at recess, a group of boys at Lockwood Street School had poked me, chanted, "Chink eyes, Chink eyes," and tugged at their eyes. At first I had ignored them, but when they persisted, I reminded them that "Chink" referred to the Chinese, not the Japanese; we were different races. A boy named LeRoy kept teasing.

"Walk away," my mother always cautioned when trouble loomed.

Walk away, my foot! This pest needed a lesson. I spun around and slammed his face with my palm, screaming, "I'm not Chinese!" I was as stunned as he was when he staggered backward and screeched, "I can't see! I can't see!"

The children gathered, eager to witness a fight. "Hit him again!" "Don't be a sissy; hit her back!" "Come on, fight!"

The playground monitor collared us and dragged us to the principal's office.

"Yuriko," Mrs. Stevens admonished, "Ladies never fight. Shame on you. And LeRoy, gentlemen never use bad names and Chink is a bad name. Now both of you say 'I'm sorry.'"

LeRoy was not blinded, but he had lost face.

For the next few weeks, I skipped recess. I pretended to read at my desk, scared of the knot of boys waiting with LeRoy by the door.

When I got my report card, I saw that red N by "gets along well with others."

"N?" my mother sighed.

"I had a little fight. A boy called me a Chink. So I hit him. He made fun of my eyes."

"What is wrong with your eyes?"

"Nothing."

Yet we both knew. American eyes were big, round, and beautiful. Japanese eyes were slanted, squinty, and ugly. Several of my mother's friends had had their eyes "fixed" with an extra eyelid fold so they appeared larger. More than once I watched as my mother gently ran a finger along her upper lid, hoping the gesture would coax another fold above her eye.

"I tell you, walk away. You shame your family," she scolded me.

"All right." I crossed my fingers behind my back.

•

When did night fall that first day on the train? We traveled hours in the tremulous light that filtered through the shades. Only when I peered out furtively did shafts of light strike me. Then, later, when I peeked, it was dark...dark inside, dark outside. I looked around. Most of the people were dozing. A few overhead lights flickered on fitfully as if loathe to awaken. I went back to sleep, cushioning my head with my jacket.

We chugged on and crossed into Arizona on day two.

Somewhere in the middle of this state, the train lurched to a stop, and two dark women heaved themselves onto our coach. We stared at these creased and bronzed apparitions. Their black braids snaked down to their hips. Silver necklaces glinted on their breasts.

"Who are they?" "Look at their clothes." "Get the police," echoed from those sitting around us. Dumbfounded, we sat and stared. Then one of the women smiled, revealing great gaps in her teeth, and boomed, "Na-va-jo. You Ha-pa-nee." She dug into a basket slung over her arm and offered squares of something puffy and brown.

"Fry bread," she said.

"That's bread?" I asked. Bread was spongy white, wrapped in waxed paper with colored dots, and had the words "Wonder Bread." These shiny puffs looked like wet cardboard.

"Eat, eat," she urged.

Were they poisoned? Were these women agents sent to kill us? I looked at my mother, but she only shrugged her shoulders. "Smells OK," she said.

I hesitated, but hunger won. I nibbled one. It oozed delicious fat.

My mother tasted one. "Ah, *oishii,* delicious," she commented.

The women walked through the car, dispensing their bread.

"One more? Plenty here."

"Yes, thank you." Both my mother and I accepted seconds.

I savored mine as the women descended into the vast desert and waved us away, arms arcing good-byes, velvet skirts swirling. They were still waving as they dissolved into the gray landscape.

"*Mah, honto ni.* Really." Were they *obake*? Ghosts?

"Where did they come from?"

"Buddha sent them. *Namu amida butsu.*"

When the train pulled away, we fell into bemused wonder. How did they know about us? Did the train really stop? Was this a dream?

I had learned about Navajo Indians in third grade. They were poor, lived in hogans, and kept flocks of sheep. They lived on reservations. Was Amache a reservation? It sounded like one. Were we destined to become another tribe in Colorado? No, the government called it a "relocation center." We were being relocated from California. But why?

We were being sent to a better camp—Mrs. Satomura had explained before we left Santa Anita—farther inland for our own safety; a better, way-better place.

"But I want to go home," I had told her.

"Not until the war is over, Yuriko."

"How long is that?"

"No one knows. Maybe a year."

"That long? Don't you want to go home?"

"We all do. Your mother said you'd visit us when we go back."

"We will."

I had stared so long at the black barracks that Mrs. Satomura had asked, "Are you all right?"

"Santa Anita is a funny home," I had replied.

•

Later that day an ancient dining car staffed by a cook and guarded by two soldiers joined the convoy. We could choose to eat in the dining car or take food back to our seats. I opted for the dining car.

In movies beaming Negro waiters in snappy white coats offered food tucked under silver domes and, with a flourish, revealed steaming roasts and quivering desserts. Eyes twinkling, Shirley Temple chirped, "Thank you, sir," and innocently added, "Sit down, sir." The Negro winked and smiled and tap-danced away. On our train, no waiters appeared. We picked up soup and sauerkraut and wieners, but we sat at a real table, not on a mess-hall bench. My father tagged along.

"Daddy, this is like home, isn't it?" I asked. That was not the exact truth. My father occasionally wavered home unsteadily to a cold dinner. One evening he arrived home and offered my mother a handful of sunflowers.

"Mrs. Nakai, these are for you," he bowed and held out the flowers.

"Mrs. Nakai? My name is Yoshiko. I'm not a stranger. I'm your wife," my mother snapped.

My father looked bewildered. "I thought you would like them."

"Mr. Nakai, please have dinner." She pointed at his plate.

My mother took the flowers, put them in a Mason jar, and centered it on the kitchen table. "Sunflowers are very bright," she said.

There was another flower story that I'd heard from my mother in bits and pieces. Working at a teletype office in Hiroshima, she saw notices from Japanese men in America seeking wives. She thought about this for a few days, then impulsively visited a hairdresser, braved a bob and a wave, sought out a photographer, and sent her photo to two of the men. A month later, she had a reply from my father.

He had family, he wrote, in Wakayama, the Nakai clan. Could she meet him there? The letter was written in florid English script, and my mother assumed that someone had written it for my father. She learned later that it was his own handwriting—he liked embellishments to the alphabet.

He enclosed two hand-tinted photographs of himself squatting among a banana tree and pineapples in Hawaii. He sported a brimmed cap, the same round, owl-eyed glasses as Junroku, my mother's brother, and a barely there smile. She puzzled about the location of the photos. What was he doing in Hawaii?

My mother was apprehensive but curious. Curious about this man who was willing to travel to Japan for a bride, and curious about America. "I will meet you," she wired back.

Her father was staggered by the news. He was barely reconciled to her move to Hiroshima. Now she was talking about leaving Japan altogether! "You understand, don't you, if you emigrate to America, you are no longer Japanese. I will have your name stricken from our family tree," he told her sternly.

She had hesitated then. But what a future might be hers in the Land of Promise, this beautiful country with "mountain majesties" and a "fruited plain."

"Father," she bowed the old-fashioned way—forehead to the floor, legs tucked under in the yoga child's pose. Then she straightened up, looked anxiously into his face, took a deep breath, and delivered her appeal: "Honorable Father, I am a good Japanese. I am a proud Japanese. I honor the emperor, I honor my family, I honor my country. But this is a big chance. We hear about America and people making successful lives there. I have discharged my duty to you, mother, Tatsuzo, Junroku, Sumiye, all my ancestors, and now it is time for me to find a life for myself. I ask your blessing." She bowed again.

Her father was silent for a minute. Then he sighed and said, "Such drama."

"What!"

"You sound like an actor in a *chanbara* movie," he chuckled. "You memorized your speech well."

"What?"

"Of course I give my blessing. I am not an *oni.*" He began to laugh. "Chanbara movie."

My mother was startled but understood the joke. Yes, she was like an actor in one of those swashbuckling samurai movies. The heroine threw herself down before the lord chamberlain or evil landowner and begged for mercy and understanding. Most often her pleas were denied.

My mother started to giggle, then—unable to control herself—to laugh with her mouth wide open, gasping for breath. Then she found herself crying and saw her father was crying, too.

"Yoshiko, my eldest child," he wept, then willed himself to control the tears. "We are both chanbara actors."

"Yes. Both of us," she nodded and wiped her tears.

So my mother and her father had gone to Wakayama City, met my father, borrowed a white Western-style wedding dress from a cousin, and the young couple had exchanged vows in an abbreviated Shinto ceremony. My father had presented her with a bouquet of flowers—my mother didn't remember what kind, except that they were white.

•

On the train, the hours dragged. Shadows flickered on the shades. Power poles darkened the veiled window, composing a duet with the clacking wheels: *swish, swash, gatan, goton.* I felt numb. People spoke only when necessary. The air was dusty, smoky.

Gatan, goton.

My mother (seated) and my father (second from the right) had this honeymoon photo taken aboard the ship that carried only my father home to America. He did not have fare for both of them and so abandoned my mother in Yokohama. She worked for a year to save enough money to follow him.

In this artificial twilight, I felt as if I were emerging once again from my tonsil surgery three years earlier. Half asleep, half awake, I had cried for water.

"No, not now," someone had whispered.

"My throat hurts."

"You'll be better soon." Again that voice.

The ether lingered. I slept, breathing in the moldy odor.

"Wake up, Yuriko," sounded that voice again as though through a fog.

"Uhhh." I couldn't open my eyes.

"You gave her too much ether," I heard my mother say. "Not good to..."

"Wake up," the other voice cut in.

"Uhhh," I grunted.

I heard shuffling footsteps, some hurried conversation, and then a man's voice: "A small fever."

I tried to open my eyes. Someone put a glass to my lips. I took a sip and was shocked when it burned my throat. I couldn't swallow.

"What's wrong?" my mother asked.

"Uhhh," I groaned again.

I fell asleep again. What was happening? I heard whispering, but the words made no sense. I dozed, then woke again and again. A hand pressed my shoulder, then touched my cheek. I floated through a chalky cloud, then plunged into a cottony pink mass. Some icy fingers wiped my brow.

When I finally awoke, my mother was still sitting by my side. Her eyes were rimmed red. She leaned toward me and whispered, "Oh, Yuriko. Oh, Yuriko."

"I want some water," I rasped.

A nurse hurried in with bowls of ice cream and Jell-O: "Eat all you want. We're glad you're awake." The ice cream tasted like ether. I pushed it away. I heard my mother murmuring softly, softly…a Buddhist prayer. It lulled me back to sleep.

I dozed again, woke up, dozed. Then through the fog, I heard my mother again. "I pray to Buddha. It can't happen again."

"Again?" I asked.

"Sumiye."

"Sumiya?"

"No, Sumiye. I named your brother after her. Such sweet baby." She hesitated. "She died so young, my sister. I will tell you later."

"Am I going to die?"

"No, no, of course not. Of course not. I'm just talking foolishly."

I went home from the hospital late that afternoon. My mother tucked me into bed, and I slept again.

On the train now, I was rocked to sleep, drugged by the hypnotic wheels.

Gatan, goton; gatan, goton.

•

Years later, my mother told me the story of her little sister, Sumiye. Her own mother had died when she was twelve, and the burden of raising her three younger siblings fell on my mother's shoulders.

Taking care of Sumiye, the youngest, who had barely turned one, was the hardest. Suddenly deprived of her mother's milk, Sumiye refused liquids until—driven by sheer hunger—she sucked at a rag soaked in barley water. My mother heard of someone who owned a cow in a neighboring village and determined to buy some milk. Early one morning she tied Sumiye on her back and set off. When Sumiye became too heavy, she set her down to toddle beside her, but her sister was diverted by every insect and plant on the pathway and stopped to inspect and play with them.

"I know that babies are curious, but I couldn't waste time," my mother told me. "I had to reach the village, then rush home to take care my brothers, make dinner. So many things to do. I dragged Sumiye, and she cried. I almost gave up, but I was so glad when we got to the farm because Sumiye drank the milk, and she smiled. That made me happy. I asked the farmer to bring milk to the temple twice a week. He asked for so much money—a cow was a rare thing then—but I told him, 'Please, I will make money somehow.'

"Mother had showed me how to make coin bags, handkerchiefs, *furoshiki,* so I took apart my mother's kimonos and worked at night. I was not a good seamstress then, but maybe people knew my story because they bought my wares. I made enough to pay the farmer and buy more vegetables. I mashed carrots and eggplant and radish and made rice gruel for Sumiye. She was always small, looked pale. I worried so much. She slept by my side, and I sang to her, told her stories every night."

As she grew older, Sumiye was an exemplary child. According to my mother, she was "pretty, compliant, studious, obedient, intelligent, cheerful, and good."

I remarked, "Like a Girl Scout. Did Sumiye skip the terrible twos?"

My mother snapped back, "Don't make fun of Sumiye. You didn't know her."

"I'm sorry," I replied. These glowing accounts of Sumiye could get tedious.

By the time Sumiye had turned five, she could read and write. My mother was seventeen when she enrolled Sumiye at the same school that she had attended so many years before, secure in the knowledge that she had tried her best and that her little sister would have the education that had been interrupted for her forever.

"I have such joy in my heart that day," she told me. "I am also—what do you say in English—'green with envy' because she gets to go to school."

My mother expected life now to be easier, happier. It was not to be.

Two years later, Sumiye woke sweating and moaning in the middle of the night. Without excuses or delay, my grandfather fetched the doctor. "He was like a demented person, crying out, praying all the way: 'Buddha, take me, not my baby. She is innocent. Let me die; let me die, not her.'" Sumiye was still breathing when the doctor arrived, but he could not save her.

"*Bachi ga att'ta,* divine retribution has hit me," my mother cried.

"*Sonna hazu wa nai,* that's not true," her father consoled her.

But my mother once again shouldered the blame. If she had taken better care of Sumiye, made an effort to feed her more nutritious food, found ways to build up her strength, her sister would have been healthier, would not have succumbed to illness. She should have taken greater heed when her mother died so unexpectedly. Sumiye was like her mother and needed extra care. She should have understood.

My mother voiced a long list of ifs and shoulds—words she carried with her as indispensable mantras for the remainder of her life. Today we'd say she exhibited a martyr syndrome; in Meiji, Japan, she was praised as being an exemplary young woman.

A wake and funeral were held for Sumiye. My mother witnessed the cremation and was the first to use the sacred chopsticks to pick up a fragment of bone and drop it into the urn. She cradled the vase tightly in her arms to the burial spot behind the temple next to their mother.

"What a bad person I was in my former life. Such bad karma. She was my baby," my mother mused even years later. "My baby. If only..."

•

Day three on the train began with grumbling: "It's been three days. How long are we going to be on this rickety train?" The policeman told us it might be another day.

As the day wore on, the air thinned to a chill. I huddled into my jacket. When I peeked out, I saw—not flat desert—but small contorted pines. I sat bolt upright, pulled the shade up, and marveled at this transformation. Even as I watched, the trees stretched taller and greener. My mother and even my father and brother stared at this spectacle.

After we began our northward trip in the middle of New Mexico, the scenery reverted to sand and brush. By day four, I wondered if we were on an endless trip, victims of some secret plot by the government to keep us forever on a train to nowhere.

I stopped the policeman and asked once again, "When do we reach Amache?"

"Today. We're headed toward Colorado now."

Today stretched into night.

For miles the train moved at a snail's pace. The landscape unfolded sand, tumbleweeds, and an occasional rocky outcropping. As the sun faded, the chug-a-chugging slowed, but we still plodded on. A sudden darkness descended. Then the train lurched and stopped with a squeal. It was so quiet that I heard the yipping of an animal outside. I held my breath.

"We're here!"—a voice broke the silence. "At last." *"Yare, yare;* well, well." "Thank goodness."

I struggled to open the window. A gush of air swept in.

What a stark landscape! Stars dotted the sky. The moon glowed upon rounded brush spreading endlessly toward the horizon. From end to end, the land seemed ready to move on its own and spill over the edge of the world. A rustling noise curled from one side and rolled to the other. An eerie wind moaned over the desert, accompanying the chatter and bustle inside the train.

"Listen, Mom," I whispered.

"What?"

"The wind."

"Wind?"

"It's singing. Listen."

"I'm too tired."

"It's weird."

"Help me get the suitcases."

"Listen for a second, Mom. Please."

Wearily my mother put her head partway out the window and said, "I hear only the wind."

"It's a song."

"Only to you."

"What do you mean?"

We sank back into our seats.

"Sometimes no one else can hear the same thing you do. You hear music. To me it's the wind," she explained.

"You sound sad."

"Yuriko," she paused. "I'm sad for you."

"For me?"

She glanced around at the commotion in the car. "I don't wish this kind of life for you, but it can't be helped. We have to *gaman*. We have to *gambaru,* take whatever life brings. You believe in music in your heart, so you hear music. I look out, and I see weeds. Inside the train, people are going crazy. Look…look at them.

"Everything is crazy because of the war. I always think of you and Sumiya first. I sacrificed everything for you and Sumiya. Finally, I think we have a decent life, that we can settle down. Life will be better. Then the war comes. Now this camp. I can't understand my bad luck. It must be *bachi.*"

"You're not responsible for the war or this camp, Mom."

"My karma."

Just then a policeman came through the train. "Attention," he announced. "Your barracks are not finished, so you'll spend one more day on the train. We're about a mile away from Granada station, where we'll disembark. We'll provide breakfast outside in the morning. Eight o'clock. We're sorry. Tomorrow you can walk around outside."

Sputtering grew into a clamor: "We want out now!" "We've been on this old junk three days!" "Let us out!" "We need air. Open the doors!"

A man banged the door. Others began stamping their feet. Fearing a stampede or else feeling sympathy, the police unlatched the door. Eager as we were, we filed out in an orderly queue as if waiting in a mess line.

The dirt was soft. After six months of trodding on asphalt, this connection with the earth sent sparks racing up my legs. I had to move, to run. I strode away from the train.

"Where are you going?" my mother asked.

"I don't know."

"Come back!"

I kept walking.

"Too dangerous," she called, stumbling after me.

As if to prove her point, a clump of sagebrush barred my path.

"What would happen if we kept walking?" I cried out.

"There's nowhere to go. Maybe we'd die." My mother took a few more steps toward me. "We must go back."

"I wish we could fly away."

My mother hesitated, then agreed, "Yes, fly away."

"What…you?"

"This life is not good. But *shikataganai*."

"Mom…?"

"Nani? What?"

"Let's see if we can reach the station. The police said that it's only a mile away."

"No. We don't know the way."

Then we heard a muffled shout. A figure ran toward us, its arms churning like a windmill. "Hey, come back. There are rattlers out there."

I pretended not to hear, but my mother had already started back toward the train.

◆

On the train—as we were settling into sleep—my mother told me a surprising story. Once she had run away from my father. She saved enough money to buy herself and my year-old brother a one-way passage to Japan.

"It took seven years—I made handkerchiefs, did housework, did sewing—but I saved it little by little," she explained. "Your daddy sometimes never came home. I was so unhappy. I could no longer *gaman*."

My mother and my infant brother, Sumiya, in 1930.
My mother has adopted American dress and bobbed hair.

Her brother wrote, rebuking her that she had forsaken Japan and the family and run off to America. No, she must not return. Her name had been stricken from the family tree, and she was no longer a member of the Iwatake clan. She wrote back that she was returning home no matter what and gave him the arrival date.

My mother sounded as if she were talking to herself. Maybe she was. I was falling asleep.

She droned on: "I went. I told myself that I could get a job if my family did not want me. I even took my sewing machine. The trip took almost a month, but Sumiya was happy on the boat because everyone paid attention to him. He was so cute. So *kawaii*. He spoke words in Japanese and English. I was so proud. Every day I was happy. I was going home, and my baby was going with me."

She was relieved to see her two brothers waiting at Yokohama. She was so glad that she almost hugged them, but she restrained herself and bowed politely. "Thank you for coming," she said. They returned the bow.

A postcard from the S.S. Kaga Maru, the liner that took my mother
and Sumiya back to Japan, where she hoped to resettle and begin a new life.

I opened my eyes and stared at her. This desire to escape—were we both
running from a situation or toward some shining ideal?

"You came back, though," I said.

"Yes, back to America."

"Why?"

She was silent.

"Why? If you were so unhappy in America."

She looked at me. "For you," she said.

"What!"

"When I went to Japan, I didn't know I was carrying you. My brothers said that one American baby and one Japanese baby would make life in Japan too hard." Her brothers convinced her that siblings ought to be the same nationality—in this case, Nisei like Sumiya. She had told them about the difference between my father, an Issei born in Japan, and his sisters, both Nisei born in America. "See," her brothers said, "they can't communicate. Brother and sisters can't talk to each other like good siblings should."

She agreed, but she had still resisted: "I told them life in America was hard, too, but they didn't understand. They think people in America are rich, have an easy life. 'You have a car'; 'you have a job,' they said. They didn't understand my suffering."

I didn't respond. What could I say? Was it my fault? Was I responsible for her grief, her unhappiness? She clutched her hard life around her like a blanket. All her life she had extolled American freedom but then wrapped herself with her ordeals like a mummy—trapping herself—to explain her trials and her bleeding heart. She was no freer in America than in the poverty-stricken countryside from which she thought she had escaped.

My mother's stay in Japan in 1931 lasted only through the summer. Determined and resolute, she returned to America. I was born early the following year and apparently caused no end of tangled problems. "You were nothing like Sumiye or even Sumiya," she remembered. "You were more like a little monkey because you were born in the Year of the Monkey. A *gasa gasa* baby from the first day."

I cried and screamed; I climbed atop furniture and wriggled under crawl spaces. I jumped from garage roofs and slid under car wheels. If my mother left a pan handle on the stove within reach, it was sure to end up on the floor or—worse—on me. If a window screen was loose, I tumbled onto the pathway outside. My knees and elbows were perpetually painted with red Mercurochrome.

When my parents were hired in the depths of the Great Depression by Harry Harrington and his wife, Carrie—my mother as housekeeper, my father as chauffeur, gardener, and houseboy—their luck changed. My parents recognized their good luck, and even my father worked conscientiously—at least for a while until his alcohol addiction proved overwhelming. The Harringtons nevertheless treated him kindly and never berated him. This was probably the first time in my father's life that he was wholeheartedly accepted just as he was. My father called Mr. Harrington Papa. Papa suggested Alcoholics Anonymous, but my father declined—he never admitted he had the disease until his liver, as well as his heart, failed him less than thirty years later. The Harringtons honored my mother's hopes to attend sewing school and helped pay part of her tuition.

Sometimes my brother and I tagged along on weekends, and because the Harringtons were childless, we became their black-haired grandchildren. Mrs. Harrington always presented us with a box of Campbell's marshmallows.

"Here you are, Prince, Yuriko. Don't eat them all at once. You'll get tummy aches," Mrs. Harrington cautioned.

If Sumiya was a prince, then I should be a princess. Maybe she saw my brother was really more royal like a prince. I was a plain Jane, nothing special.

"Thank you very much. We won't."

I ate one as she expectantly watched. The gooey puffballs stuck to my teeth and oozed lazily into my throat as if unwilling to be absorbed. I preferred the chocolate bonbons displayed in the sunken living room. Sometimes if I lingered long enough by them, Mrs. Harrington offered one with her usual admonition: "Chew carefully." Holding my prize, I sank into the brocaded sofa, whooshing the air out of the cushion and, yes, nibbling daintily so the candy lasted and lasted. When I stood up, the cushion swelled into a loaf again.

"Awk, awk. Polly want a cracker," a parrot shrieked by the back door. It screeched two other phrases: "Hello, darling; hello, darling," and "Oh, you beautiful doll, you great big beautiful doll," and repeated them indiscriminately. I thought it was very smart. I asked Mrs. Harrington if it ever left its cage.

"Let me show you," she said. She unlatched the door. The parrot shot past me and flew up the winding staircase.

"Where is it going?"

"Why don't you follow?"

I climbed the stairs and found the parrot perched on Mr. Harrington's shoulder. He was sitting in an armchair shuffling a deck of cards on a card table—not an ordinary one but one with ornately carved wooden legs and a soft beige suede cover. Mr. Harrington wore a shiny dark red bathrobe. The room smelled of Mentholatum, caramel, and tobacco.

"Here," he offered, "have a caramel. You look skinny." I took one.

"What if the parrot does his thing on you?" I asked.

"That's why I have this towel." He pointed to his shoulder.

"No one else I know owns a parrot."

"I was going to teach him to talk. Then he and I could have conversations. Wouldn't that be fun? When Yoshiko and Ken came to work for us, I tried to teach him Japanese, but he couldn't learn. *Ohayou, ohayou,* good morning, good morning; *konnichiwa, konnichiwa,* how are you?, how are you? He's too old to learn, I suspect."

"They can't really talk, Mr. Harrington. They just repeat stuff."

"I know that, dear."

"How do you know it's a he?"

"Hmmmm, I'm not sure. I brought it back from Siam."

"Siam?"

"Yes, dear. That's in Asia, the other side of the world."

The Harringtons' house seemed far from ours. I guessed that Asia, Japan, and Siam were even farther.

"Do you live upstairs?" I asked him. I'd never seen Mr. Harrington downstairs.

"I can't walk up and down stairs."

"How come?"

"I was hurt in the war, dear."

"Don't you ever go outside? I could push you in your wheelchair."

"No, dear. Mrs. Harrington takes me onto the balcony every day. I can see everything from there."

"Don't you get bored?"

"No, dear. Would you like to learn how to shuffle cards?"

"Yes!" I said. "Yes, please." He'd already taught Sumiya, who then taunted me about my lousy card skills. This was my chance. I'd show him now.

So for the next hour, Mr. Harrington taught me riffling and then solitaire. The parrot perched quietly on Mr. Harrington's shoulder and watched. He didn't squawk; he didn't poop.

I went downstairs. Mrs. Harrington called the parrot, and he swooped back into his cage.

I walked into the dining room. Gleaming red goblets posed proudly in a cupboard. They took my breath away.

"They are so…so red." Did I sound stupid? No wonder she didn't address me as a princess.

"They create that deep color by adding real gold, Yuriko. Would you like to hold one?" Mrs. Harrington asked.

"No, thank you. I'll just look. I don't want to drop it."

"Someday you'll have ruby glasses in a big house, too," she told me.

"You think so?"

"I'm sure of it."

TAIHEIYO SEWING SCHOOL

My mother graduated in 1936 from sewing school. Her graduation photo shows twenty-three women clad in identical white dresses with dark buttons and scarves neatly tucked into their collars. "Red buttons and scarves," my mother said. "I wanted blue, but everyone else wanted red like the Japanese flag."

This photograph disappeared during the war years, then reappeared on the bedroom walls of all my mother's subsequent homes—a flagship symbol of a huge step in her life. I hardly glanced at it as a child, but as I neared my own high-school graduation, I found myself scrutinizing it for…what? I was struck by the enormity of my mother's accomplishment, her resolve and tenacity. Her goal for an education was life altering; mine was just an expected step toward college.

My mother watched me perusing the photograph. "Don't we look like—how you say it—robots?" she asked.

"No, you're all individuals, Mom, and you're the prettiest," I answered, not to flatter her but because it was true. No wonder my father had chosen her.

Why don't we describe our parents in terms of beauty? We're so busy negating their attempts at enforcing propriety and regulations that they become symbols of authority. We bunch them together with policemen, teachers, politicians. They're all stern and severe. I never looked—really looked—at my mother until she was old and wrinkled. I realized then she must have been gorgeous as a teenager with her regular features and strong bones. She used makeup until Alzheimer's left her unable to remember what the eyebrow pencil—that chunky blue one that she sharpened with a paring knife—was for.

"Pretty? Your daddy called me *uma*. Horse. Horse face because I have a square face."

I looked at her. "Yeah, but horses neigh. Can you neigh?" I joked.

"You're making fun?"

I changed the subject. "The students were all Japanese?"

"Of course. We Japanese could not attend white schools, so our teacher formed her own school, the Taiheiyo Sewing School. We had all crossed the Taiheiyo, Pacific Ocean, to attend this school. She was very proud, very strict. I thank her often for teaching me well."

•

At her graduation, I recall the banks of flowers that surrounded the stage. Their stifling fragrance was overpowering. A congratulatory dinner followed the ceremony. One special event was a raffle. The tickets were free, and even the children were given one. When the final number was drawn, it was mine! I claimed my prize, but the lady clutching the small oblong box peered at me and hesitated. My mother hurried to my side. "So sorry, but Yuriko and I must have mixed up our tickets. That one is mine," she stated with great authority. The lady smiled and handed the box to my mother.

A group photograph of the graduates of the Taiheiyo Sewing School.
My mother is the third woman from the left in the top row.

I won this fan in a raffle at the Taiheiyo Sewing
School graduation dinner. The five cranes
symbolize happiness, long life, and good luck.

At our table, my mother gave me the box. "Here, Yuri-chan, you open it." I wasn't certain what had just happened—why hadn't I gotten the prize?—but I opened the wooden box, and nestled within lay a golden fan stamped with five pairs of stylized cranes. "Oh…so wonderful," my mother crooned. I held the fan up. The crowd of women agreed: "Beautiful." "You must treasure that." "Cranes are good luck."

My mother's sewing activities and my father's absence dominate my memories during those childhood years leading to World War II. Women—never men—arrived at our house in their sleek cars and hurried into the fitting room, actually the bedroom. The women stood on a hollow box constructed by my father that allowed my mother to kneel below and pin up their skirt hems. "Please turn slowly," my mother directed, and dutifully the women took baby steps round and round until the skirt bottoms glittered with pins. "Umm, this side, please," my mother urged and repinned a tiny section, stepping back to peer at the edge. Sometimes the woman became impatient: "It looks fine in the mirror, Mrs. Nakai," she said.

"Must be perfect. Anything I sew must be perfect," my mother replied.

This perfection earned her a steady clientèle. If a client brought a store pattern, my mother altered the design into a custom fit. She created easy methods of sewing bound buttonholes and inserting zippers. For each problem she encountered, she found a solution. She drafted and constructed suits and overcoats that equaled any found in department stores.

Often I accompanied her to a client's home. She swooped up her ready-to-go sewing paraphernalia, and we sped away in her car. *Her* car. It clanked and rattled as much as my father's panel truck, but it was all hers. After her return from Japan, she pinched nickels and dimes and—within a year or two—triumphantly drove home this automobile. "Even your daddy liked it," she told me. "He said it was a good car and he would help fix it if there was trouble. I think he was little jealous. We went for a drive and honked at people we knew, and even some we didn't know. Everyone waved back. He took me to a Chinese restaurant for dinner. See, your daddy could be nice like that," she concluded wistfully.

These forays into clients' homes impressed me with their foreign smells. The hallways bloomed with a tang of dried flowers and floor polish; in the living room, the scent of fresh blossoms mingled with the dust of heavy brocade drapes. And, oh, their kitchens! Their kitchens were heaven scented. I tiptoed into those vast spaces where stews bubbled and cookies baked, engulfing me with their aromas. While my mother pinned and directed—"Please raise your right arm; thank you,"—I drew in deep breaths so that the odors would soak into my pores and brain. These were authentic American smells. If I could infuse our house with these smells, I'd be genuinely American. After the visits, I willed myself to recall these scents, but almost always they evaporated before we even reached the car. We went home to our Japanese smells—sandalwood, incense, steaming rice, and laundry starch.

The bedrooms—some women called them "boudoirs"—were permeated by heady perfumes seductively lined up on dressing tables in glistening glass bottles. At home my mother's dresser displayed Pond's cold cream and Coty Airspun face powder in the Rachel shade but not an ounce of cologne or perfume. I treasured those Coty boxes with white puffs of cotton floating in an orange sky on their covers; my mother surrendered them to me once they were empty. The scent lingered for years.

One client noticed my keen interest in her bottles and offered me a tiny empty one, but my mother declined. "Thank you very much," she said. "It is too beautiful to give away. Besides, Yuri-chan is too young."

Too young? Speak for yourself, Mama, I thought.

The woman pressed the bottle into my mother's hand. "Then, please, you take it."

But my mother returned it to the dressing table.

Later, I complained loudly.

My mother then explained one of her "facts of life" to me: "Yuriko, you must understand. People don't give away precious things without expecting something in return. If we took the bottle, the lady would expect some favor from me. Next time we go to Kress, I will buy a bottle for you."

"People are like that?" I asked.

"Yes. I found out the hard way. I don't want you to be hurt."

"Well, OK, then," I replied. By our next trip to the five-and-dime store, I had forgotten about the bottles. Her fact of life, however, remained imprinted on my brain. It was many years before I learned that occasionally people gave from the heart without any expectations.

◆

As a child, I didn't realize how fortunate I was to have a dressmaker for a mother. Whenever I asked for a dress, my mother found time to make it— and make it from scratch. I told her my idea, she sketched a design, drafted a pattern, and carefully, perfectly, constructed it. One summer my friend Sachiko appeared in a long housecoat. Housecoats were meant to be indoor wraps—to fling on while dusting furniture or after a bath—so flaunting them outdoors was the epitome of daring. I had to have one. And, no, no, thank you, not a *yukata,* not one of those cotton kimonos. I wanted an American-style robe that swirled around my ankles.

My mother went to work. In a few days I joined Sachiko in my new housecoat, and we paraded up and down Commonwealth Avenue feeling very grown up. We soon had a contingent of girls clad in long skirts following us. We asked our mothers and older friends for old high-heeled shoes and hats and staggered like drunkards in single file to the beat of an imaginary band.

I had another very special dress. I fell in love with Snow White's gown, set off by huge puffed sleeves with tear-dropped insets and a pointy waist. Her skirt billowed in the movie, surrounding her like a cloud.

"Mama, Mama, please, please," I begged, "I really, really have to have a dress like hers."

"So complicated...," she replied.

"Please, oh, please."

"It will take a little time. Maybe for Halloween?"

"Yes, yes, yes."

A week before Halloween, I waved this dress like a flag, showing it off to some friends in my front yard. The bodice was dark blue velvet; the sleeves, red. The skirt rippled like ocean waves. It was perfect. It was beautiful. Suddenly, a gust of wind tugged it from my hands and flung it into the driveway just as my father drove up. I sprinted to retrieve my precious gown, but too late—crunch, splat—the front wheels of his truck flattened it, and then, even worse, as I tugged at it, I slipped and fell beneath the truck, and a back wheel spun over my legs.

Totally focused on the gown, I sprang up, grabbed the skirt, and burst into tears. It was torn...ripped! My Snow White gown...ruined. It was only when I tried to run inside to show my mother that I realized my legs hurt. I looked down. Tread marks dotted my shins.

My father swooped me up and carried me to the house, yelling, "Mama, Mama!"

Strangely, as soon as I felt my father's arms cradling me, the pain stopped. Even when the doctor examined my legs while I lay on the sofa, there was only an achy pressure. "Lucky, no broken bones," he said. "Be more careful next time."

The following day wide bruises laced my legs. My father—*my father*—stayed home that day and brought me cold washcloths. He sped to the corner grocery store and returned with Hostess cupcakes, the kind with dark chocolate frosting topped by white squiggles. He brought me extra pillows and blankets and—for the first time in my life—read me a bedtime story. I don't remember what it was, but I still hear the cadence of his voice dipping and rising, droning on as I fell asleep. That was the first and last story he ever read to me. Perhaps I should have manufactured more accidents.

My mother didn't have time to sew another Snow White dress, but a few months later, she surprised me with a frothy, dotted-with-red-spots white dress. The sleeves and skirt were ruffled in layers that fluttered like butterflies. I became a butterfly. I whirled and danced in this dress and performed a solo for Grandmother Nakai. *Why was my grandmother here alone with me? It must have been one of those rare occasions when she had agreed to watch me while my mother was gone. Though she lived in a carbon-copy house next door for a few years, I seldom saw her.* I so wanted to please her. I pranced on tiptoes and spun across the room. She clapped, and I coaxed a tiny, tiny smile from her.

"You must become a dancer, Yuri-chan, when you grow up," she praised.

When we unpacked our trunks at Amache, the dress was there.

"I know you can't wear it anymore, but maybe you can give it to your own child some day," my mother explained. "What do you call it…as an heirloom?"

I searched for the dress after we moved to Salt Lake City, a few years before the basement flooded. It was gone. When I asked my mother about it, she said she had sent it to Japan.

"What! You told me it was an heirloom for your grandchild!"

"Reiko sent a letter telling me that the *bakudan,* the bomb, had destroyed everything in Hiroshima. Babies, children had no clothes, no food. Nothing. People were trying to rebuild. To please send anything I had."

"Cousin Reiko's my age, Mom. The dress would be way too small."

"Yes, but maybe other young *kodomo* could wear it. Poor children. I saw pictures in magazines, newspapers. Reiko and her family were far enough from the bomb center, so they were OK, but she was helping other victims."

"Why didn't you ask me first, Mom?"

"I'm sorry; I didn't think. I packed in a hurry. I sent your blue kimono and obi, too. All my extra dresses. I even bought new fabric. I sent food, candy."

So what could I say? That the kids deserved the A-bomb? It was their karma? Too bad—they were in the wrong place at the wrong time?

"That's OK, Mom. You did a good thing. I'm glad you sent it," I said to comfort her.

Who wore my ruffled dress? Did you dance and twirl; did you prance and bow? Did you listen to the music in your head and glide to the tune? Oh, my Japanese friend, did you love the dress?

I did.

•

That first night on the train in Colorado was as strange as the first one in Santa Anita. No searchlights this time. No clicking footsteps. The night was hushed as if wrapped in velvet. The wind swished and crooned as it rolled over the brush. Some people slept outside on the ground. My father and brother took advantage of the empty seats and stretched out. The stars were brilliant, the air so clear that they seemed to hover in the inky-blue sky. In the distance, coyotes began to yelp. One…two…then answering calls. Finally, a chorus. Their eerie howls pitched back and forth, and I fell asleep to their moans.

Many years later—when my mother was so feeble she could no longer feed herself—I coaxed a spoonful of oatmeal between her lips and asked, "Mom, do you remember that night when we got off the train at Amache and thought about running away?"

"I went to Japan," she mumbled.

"Remember that night? What would have happened if we had walked away?"

PHOENIX RISING, WATERCOLOR, 22 BY 30 INCHES.
The phoenix, a symbol of hope, rises from the Genbaku Dome, the only structure left standing
after the A-bomb was dropped on Hiroshima. Today it stands in the Hiroshima Peace Park as a poignant reminder
of the devastation. My mother sent care packages to my cousins who lived in the Hiroshima area.

"I went to Japan," she repeated.

"We went to Amache, Mom."

"Japan. I went to Japan."

I reached for her hand the way I had in Santa Anita and held it. I didn't contradict her.

BLOCK 9L, AMACHE

As promised by the policeman on the train, breakfast was at eight. I don't remember what we ate. I breathed in the herbal tang of the sagebrush and ate sand with my food.

"This is camping in the wild," I said to no one in particular and giggled at my private joke.

The women asked for water and tubs to wash themselves and their grimy clothes. Some accepted a ride in truck beds to a laundry facility in the completed compound. They were gone all day. When they returned, we greeted them with a babble of questions: "Does it look like Santa Anita?" "Are there lots of people?" "Where did you wash your clothes?" "Are there guard towers?"

We learned that Amache had a laundry and bathroom for every twelve barracks. Those twelve barracks formed a block. Each block had a mess hall. The lunch the women had been given was identical to the ones at Santa Anita, but the lines were shorter. And the barracks were different—not black like those we'd left behind but tan, as though they were covered in sheets of sandpaper, they told us.

That image was not far from reality. Three days later, after a third night on the train, I dragged my suitcase up an incline toward our new "home." We passed barracks with rough pebbly surfaces that merged with the desert as if they were camouflaged. In the distance, a checkered orange-and-white water tank perched on spindly legs.

"I can't pull my suitcase over this bumpy dirt. The truck could have brought us closer," I griped. No one answered. Secretly I was fascinated by the sere surroundings, but it seemed inappropriate to gush over cactus and sagebrush while other people, frowning and sweating, complained about it.

My mother and brother hurried ahead. My father plodded behind.

I stopped in front of a wooden shed. "What's this?" I hollered.

"Go see," my brother yelled back.

I pulled on the door.

"Come on in," a voice sang.

I jumped back in surprise. My brother doubled over with laughter.

"That's not funny. Who's in there?" I demanded.

I opened the door by inches, expecting one of my brother's friends to leap out crying "boo!" Instead, a woman sat on a plank. Two holes gaped in the wood next to where she sat. "Come in," she repeated.

I slammed the door, picked up my suitcase, and caught up to my brother.

"It's a toilet!" I cried.

"Outhouse," he corrected me. He was still snickering.

"Is that where we're going to...you know...?"

"I guess so," he shrugged.

"I don't believe it."

"Don't."

I glanced back at my father. I waited for him to catch up. "Did you see the *benjo*? I'm not going to use a stinky outhouse! How long do you think we'll be here?"

"I will leave as soon as I can," my father said solemnly.

"What do you mean?"

"Some places in the East are giving work to the Japanese."

"They are?"

"Yes. Anywhere is better than here."

Here was Block 9L, Building 9, Apartment C, my address for the next three and a half years. The room was slightly larger than the one at Santa Anita. A potbellied stove squatted in one corner. Four metal beds filled half the floor space. One bare bulb hung in the center of the ceiling. The floor was made of bricks set atop the dirt. Again we hauled our blankets and pillows from a storehouse, only this time my father helped. His willingness once more surprised me.

I discovered yet-another side of my father when two trunks arrived a month later from Los Angeles. He watched as my mother struggled to lift a

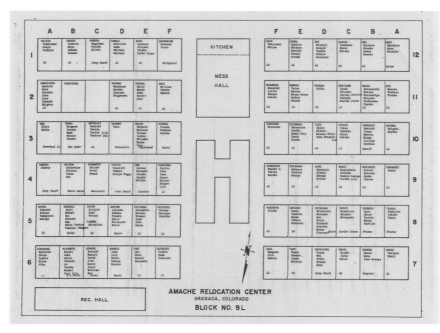

The layout of Block 9L.

The Amache directory, listing the Nakai family on page 87.

中川 健三 Nakagawa, Kenzo	和歌山縣和哥山市三町目	農	11F-Rec.	55	Yuba City, Calif.
中川 茂六 Nakagawa, Moroku	廣嶋縣安佐郡三入村	農	11F-11E	64	Napa, Calif.
中川 新太郎 Nakagawa, Shintaro 妻 Ritsu, Yutaka, Kei, Akiko, Kimiko	和歌山縣西牟婁郡和深村	漁業	6E-7E	55	Terminal Island, Calif.
中川 忠明 Nakagawa, Tadaaki 妻 June, Jean, Tad, Ronald	米國	農	10H-8C	31	P.O. Box 5. Livingston, Calif.
中川 竹次郎 Nakagawa, Takejiro 妻 Kiku, Hideo, Torajiro, Saburo, Seshiro, Akio, Mitsuko, Setsuyo	山口縣萩市沖原村	農	9K-5C	63	Hawaii
中川 徹雄 Nakagawa, Tetsuzo 妻 Gladys	広島県山口町	商	8G-2E	66	306 C Marysville, Calif.
中川 卯一 Nakagawa, Uichi 妻 Chisa, Hiromu	山口縣大島郡安下庄村	農	12F-1F	58	Rt. 2, Box 346 Sebastopol, Calif.
中口 博 Nakaguchi, Hiroshi	和歌山縣海草郡楠見村	農	12H-10D	23	Los Angeles, Calif.
中隈 末次郎 Nakaguma, Suejiro 妻 Mitsuyo, Michitaka, Yoshitatsu, Dojun	福岡縣三井郡宮ノ津村	農	6H-5C	74	P.O. Box 757 Woodland, Calif.
中井 兼三郎 Nakai, Kanesaburo 妻 Yoshiko, Sumiya, Yuriko	和歌山縣海草郡安原村	庭園業	9L-5C	45	1253 No.Commonwealth Los Angeles, Calif.
中井 楠右エ門 Nakai, Kusuemon 妻 Fusa	和歌山縣海草郡安原村		11K-3A	68	N. Commonwealth Hollywood, Calif.
中井 茂 Nakai, Shigeru 妻 Masa, Shigeko, Robert, Hisashi, Midori	三重縣名賀郡上津村	農	8E-4B	43	P.O. Box 426 Winters, Calif.
中居 三吉 Nakai, Sankichi	鹿児島縣大島郡喜界村	料理人	6F-4C	44	Tacoma, Wash.

GUILT IS A FORM OF SUPPRESSED ANGER, WATERCOLOR, 22 BY 30 INCHES.
So many Issei (first-generation Japanese) could only sigh shikataganai, "it can't be helped," and gaman, "persevere,"
in accepting their fate, whatever that might be. I wondered what their true feelings were, especially about their forced
incarceration. This angry woman is spearing a Buddhist god.

box from one. A sudden gleam lit up his eyes, and he rushed to help her. He hauled out a simple plywood toolbox and set it on the floor.

"You…," he stuttered, "you…packed this?"

"Maybe you can use it here," my mother answered and turned quickly away.

My father stroked the wooden lid thoughtfully, then opened it and took out a heavy chisel. He grasped it tightly and waved it in the air as if testing its weight.

"Hey, are these yours?" I asked. I was incredulous. My father a carpenter? I'd never seen this box of tools. He dislodged a huge screwdriver, easily more than a foot long.

"What's that used for?" I asked.

"Big screws," he said.

"I know, but what did you make using that?"

He dismissed the question. "Tomorrow I'll look for wood," he said simply.

For the next few hours, he sat on his bed and inscribed each tool with a penknife. He carved his initials, K. N., or his surname, Nakai.

"Everyone will know these are mine," he declared.

"Won't they take that knife away if the big shots find it?"

"They won't find it," he said with simple conviction. "Besides, the rules are different here."

The next day I tagged along on his foray to the camp dump. The pickings were few. Internees had scavenged usable scraps; we found only unusable discards.

"I'll find something," my father said, and after a few days, he brought home some plywood scraps and two-by-fours.

"Where did you find those?" I asked, but he only shrugged and began measuring the wood.

"What are you making?"

"A screen. Then we'll have a bedroom."

"I want to help."

Without interrupting his work, he mumbled, "You can hammer this."

I was so convinced he would say no that I had taken a step toward the door. He pushed a hammer toward me and showed me where to pound in the nails.

We worked in silence for a while.

"Dad, are you going back East? I heard that men are leaving to work."

My father continued to saw: *Whoosh, whoosh.*

"Can't you stay?"

"No good jobs in camp. I can make more on the outside."

He zipped out a metal tape and penciled a line.

I tried again. "Dad, maybe you can make partitions and sell them."

He didn't answer.

"People want privacy and…"

"My ears hurt when you talk so much," he said.

"We never get to…"

"You make my ears hurt."

"We don't need a lot of money. Mom is going to work…" I stopped when he wrinkled his brow and glared. So he sawed, and I hammered until I got bored—bored with the silence and the repetitious work. I left him to his thoughts and his labor.

•

And indeed my mother did work; she became a sewing teacher. Her students addressed her as *"sensei,* teacher." Teacher! Teachers were objects of reverence, of admiration, and smiling, she wore her stature like a badge. My father had no hold over her new life here. He was unable to control even the smallest details. She became sensei, and he was relegated to the husband of the teacher. Nudged by her insistence, I became part of her class. "One day you will be glad," she said.

Because all the students were Nisei women, my mother taught in English—grammatically correct and precise, the way she had learned in that class located by the Maryknoll nursery school long before. I had heard her converse with her dressmaking customers and Mrs. Harrington in English,

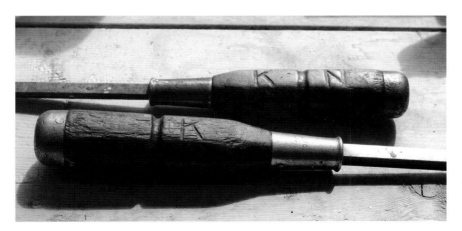

My father's screwdrivers, which he carefully inscribed with his initials.
They were very precious to him.

but now I understood the earnestness with which she had studied this second language.

"We shall learn to draft simple basic patterns first in quarter size; then later you will all have a chance to make a pattern of your choice," she explained. "I want you to find a picture of a dress style you like, and, by the time we finish this class, you will be able to draft and make it."

A chorus of "oohs" followed her little speech.

From a Montgomery Ward catalog, we ordered drawing pads. The students praised me as I handed them out: "Oh, thank you, Yuriko; you're so mature coming to this class." "I wish my daughter had come, too." "You must be proud of your mother."

I was pleased. My mother blushed. "Oh, what are you saying?" she asked shyly.

My mother found some pattern books in a heap donated to the camp. I carefully cut out a figure clad in a sheer flowing dress. The sleeves formed inverted Vs, fluttering in an invisible breeze. "Let's make this one," I suggested.

"Later. Today we will make plain and puffed sleeves."

The next lesson was skirts, straight and gored. Then a basic blouse, a baby's sundress, a man's shirt.

"I want to draft this dress," I tried again weeks later.

"That design is too hard for a first one. Besides, we cannot get the lace for the bodice because of the war." She pushed the pattern books toward me. "See if you can find another one."

Disappointed, I muttered, "Dumb war."

"Yuriko!"

"She's right, Mrs. Nakai, the war is dumb," a white-haired lady agreed. "Look what's happened to us. I never dreamed I'd be living in the middle of a God-forsaken desert."

Another student cut in: "My father is old and confused. Every day he walks to the gate to wait for a bus to take him home to Mama. She's been gone for ten years. The guards give him food. Then he sits there until I get him. 'Good-bye, Mr. Sato, see you tomorrow. The bus is sure to come then,' the guards say. My father smiles and bows to them. Bows to the soldiers; can you imagine?"

A woman put her arm around the woman's shoulder. "Mrs. Nakai, one good thing about camp is that I get to come to your class," she said.

"Yes," another woman agreed. "It's hard here, but I'm excited because I'm learning something new—pattern drafting. I'd never have this chance on the farm. You're such a good teacher."

Another compliment. My mother blushed and shuffled her papers. "Um...we must continue our lesson."

We picked up our pencils.

An outside group donated four Singer sewing machines. We constructed clothes from our patterns. My mother's salary was sixteen dollars a month, and we used part of that to order fabric from Monkey Ward, our nickname for Montgomery Ward, replacing what was a real tongue twister for native Japanese speakers. We ordered by description—the catalog was in black and white. When my yardage arrived, the color was lighter than I expected, but I lied: "I love this."

My mother glanced at me and said, "Yes, my cloth is good, too."

At the end of the class, we wore our creations. My simple blouse draped fluidly, and the aqua hue was perfect after all.

"You were right, Mom. I'm glad I came to class with you."

"See, I told you."

"Yes, you did."

•

I was isolated from the real world, but letters linked me to the outside. Marlene, my school friend—not a friend friend—sent chatty notes. After school in Los Angeles, we used to walk to the gate together, then part, even though we shared the sidewalk for a block. One day a tall blond girl passed by as Marlene and I chatted in the hall at school. I had seen her before; she was a popular, sunny girl, usually surrounded by a clutch of giggling girls. Today she was alone, and as she passed by, she muttered, "Jap-ass." We ignored her. The girl stopped and asked me, "Aren't you a Jap? My father said you Japs look like monkeys."

I was stunned. With the speed of a lioness whose cubs had been threatened, Marlene stepped between the girl and me and clipped, "Don't say that. Don't ever say that again." I'll never forget the look of astonishment on the girl's face as she sputtered, "No one, ever…," Marlene repeated, a little louder this time, "Never again." The girl, flustered, backed away and hurried down the hall.

I had never witnessed such bravery. I should have said thank you, but I didn't know how. We just continued into art class. We were friends because we had assigned seats next to each other. She said my name was pretty. I told her it meant "lily" in Japanese, and we spent the hour drawing lilies. I signed one with a flourish and presented it to her; she gave me one of hers. I wanted to be friends with her forever.

In her first letter, Marlene wrote that she had been assigned to take my place as weekly flower attendant—meaning she discarded the wilted flowers from a vase. "I washed out that slimy green stuff. Ugh. How did you stand it?" she asked.

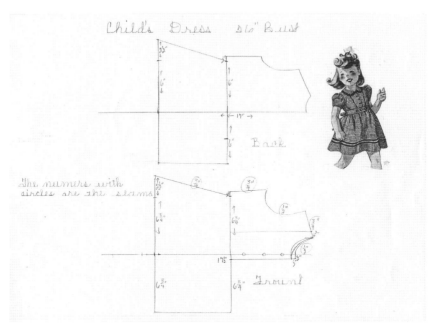

My drafting pattern, created in my mother's sewing class at Amache.

I wrote back, "I breathed through my mouth. But I love that vase."

She replied, "You love a vase?"

I did. Its glass rectangles sprinkled rainbows across the walls when I slanted it in the light. On alternate Mondays, the teacher tucked new flowers into the vase.

One day I noticed that the stems zigzagged in the water and asked the teacher why that was so. She explained it was refraction and suggested I try drawing it.

I stared at the stems and drew straight lines—slash—into the water. Then I added crooked lines and more shattered lines. I concentrated and penciled delicate ripples for water, dark strokes for shadows. The teacher praised the sketch and urged me to draw the flowers.

I stared at the blossoms. The petals were ruffled. Too hard to copy, so I drew circles instead—lots of them. Balls and bubbles overlapping, popping, sinking. I carefully shaded them in gorgeous pastel colors.

"Oh, what have you done? You've spoiled your picture," the teacher exclaimed.

"No, no, it's a forest for fairies."

"That was not what I asked you to do. Start over and try to draw the flowers correctly. I'll come help."

I began again but drew squiggles and wriggly lines. When the bell rang, I crumpled both pictures and threw them into the wastebasket.

Marlene's correspondence continued for a few months, but we found nothing more in common to write about. I didn't want to hear about her trip to the ocean…oh, how I longed for the swirl of seaweed tangling around my ankles. Or about the passion flowers climbing on the west wall of the school…we used to wait days for a blossom to disclose its spiny stamens, hoping that no one would pick the flower before it unfurled. Or how she could reach the dangling metal rings in the playground in a single jump. I had no tales of wonder, only of the desert and mess meals.

I mailed penny postcards to movie stars and requested autographed photos. The usual reply was "please enclose twenty-five cents to defray the cost of mailing and handling." I didn't have the money. Elizabeth Taylor was my heroine because she and I were the same age and we both had black hair. I explained my situation to her:

> Dear Miss Taylor,
>
> I know you are supposed to send a quarter for an autographed photo, but I don't have it because I live in a relocation camp in Colorado. I would appreciate your response. I admire your acting very much.
>
> Sincerely yours

Miss Taylor never replied. For years I followed her fortunes. The *Los Angeles Times* announced that her new film, *Lassie Come Home,* was a sensation. I waited six years to see the movie in a rerun and was surprised that Lassie struggled home to Roddy McDowall. In my imagination, Elizabeth

Taylor was the sobbing owner—reunited at last, speechless with joy—with her bedraggled collie.

I wrote another fan letter:

> Dear Miss Taylor,
>
> You are absolutely the best actress in the world. I was able to see your film, *Lassie Come Home,* only recently. You were terrific in *National Velvet.*

This time, however, I didn't hope for a reply. I just wanted her to know.

·

School in Amache convened in a barrack two blocks from mine. In cramped rows, we huddled at old desks scarred by initials and hearts carved into their tops. The gaping hole for inkwells made a perfect target for scraps of paper or sometimes a secret note. A weekly highlight was a spelling test. On Monday we copied words to study. On Friday we followed precise instructions for the test: "Tear a sheet of paper in half down the middle. Write your name neatly at the top left. Write 1 to 10 with a period after each number."

After the test, we traded copies with another student, checked the spelling as Mrs. Bender recited the words, circled misspelled words, wrote the number of correct answers at the right-hand top, and returned the test to the owner. When Mrs. Bender asked those of us who got 10s to raise our hands, almost all the hands went up. This was because if someone misspelled a word, the corrector fixed it before returning the test. The only time we didn't cheat was to get back at someone. Mrs. Bender never caught on. Or so we thought.

"Very good. You are all such wonderful spellers," she beamed.

One day—rather than have us trade papers with another student—she asked that we send them to the front. As she gathered them up, she announced, "Penmanship is so important. This spelling test will give me a sample of your handwriting, and tomorrow we'll have a penmanship lesson. All of you will learn beautiful cursive writing."

We never cheated after that day.

•

At home in California, the weather was perfect all year, and I loved being outdoors more than anywhere else. But here in Colorado, that soon began to change. Recess was twice a day, at 10:00 a.m. and 2:00 p.m.

"Everyone outside. You must get sunshine every day," Mrs. Bender directed. No urging needed with me. I bolted from the room.

Then one afternoon ominous gray air blotted the sun. In a matter of seconds, a dust storm blasted in. We didn't go outside.

The dust and sand whistled through the cracks, coating the floor and desks. We coughed and wheezed. My eyes burned. My mouth filled with grit.

I wiped a window and peered out. A roiling brown cloud whooshed across the pane, eclipsing the barrack only a few yards away.

"I'll dismiss school early as soon as the wind dies down," Mrs. Bender said in a tight voice.

The wind kept blowing. The air became thicker.

"What are we going to do, Mrs. Bender? It's not stopping," someone asked.

"It will be over soon," Mrs. Bender replied.

We waited.

Sand rasped against the windows, sounding like mice scratching for shelter. It spun in around the window frame, mounded on the sill, then streamed to the floor, where it puffed into hills. *What if the sand and dust blew in all night? What if they kept coming and coming and buried us? We'd smother to death. We would try to claw our way out of the choking mounds the way those ants must have tried when we poured dirt into their mazes. "Oh, those poor ants, those poor children! How they must have suffered," the*

SEA OF DUST, WATERCOLOR, 22 X 30 INCHES.
Amache was at the edge of a dust bowl. The dust storms were fierce and there was no escape.

mourners would lament. I shook my head to get rid of this daydream. I realized I was very thirsty.

"It's getting dark," another student ventured. "I want to go home."

"Yes, but we'll wait a few minutes longer." Mrs. Bender's voice wavered.

We sat in the gloom. Someone started to cry. I didn't turn to look. I was afraid I'd cry, too.

"What time is it, Mrs. Bender?" I asked. My lips felt glued together.

Just then we heard raps on the door, and two men blew in with a blast of dust. They looked like ghosts. "The lights are out! We need to get you kids outta here," one blurted.

"Dad!" Sumi cried. Her father had braved the storm to rescue her, to rescue us.

"Ah, Sumi-chan." "Hold hands. Make a chain, Mrs. Bender at the end. We'll lead you to Terry Hall, then home," he told us. He handed Mrs. Bender a flashlight.

We grabbed hands that were grimy with sweat and dust and stepped into the storm, leaning into the wind and trying frantically to stay upright. Sand scraped my face and arms. I scrunched my eyes, peering at the shoes in front of me and following blindly. "Keep going; we're almost there," Sumi's father encouraged, his voice barely audible.

Banks of candles sputtered in Terry Hall. Some Coleman lanterns sat dark on desks, their mantles having given up the struggle against shifting drafts of wind. Opaque light strained through the windows. Children hunkered on the floor or slumped on folding chairs. Heads on their knees, arms wrapped around their legs, they looked like baby bears settling in for winter in their caves. We took turns sipping cloudy water from a bucket. It tasted like mud.

"We'll start by taking kids home who live the farthest," one man said.

I settled against a wall.

Terry Hall had originally been built as a mess hall but now served as our auditorium and the place where Protestants and Catholics held church services. A large wooden cross, bigger than a man, leaned in the gloom next to me. A dais, the pulpit, stood guard beside it.

My friend Helen's family embraced Christianity. Before the war, she had invited me to a service at her cathedral. Light streamed through stained-glass windows, mottling the congregation. The pastor preached about sin and redemption…man was evil…he must be saved. "Pray, pray for salvation."

I told Helen I didn't know any Christian prayers.

"Just say anything. It doesn't need to be a real prayer. God will forgive you," Helen said.

"Anything? Like what?"

"Something that sounds religious, like 'holy' and 'confession.'"

So that's what I whispered: "Holy confession, God and father, holy confession."

I was intrigued and intimidated by the figure of Christ slumped on a splintered cross, blood seeping from his hands and feet. I glanced furtively at it, afraid that some evil would descend if a non-Christian stared too long at this holy man.

After the service, Helen asked if I wanted to come again, but I declined and told her that her church was scary. It contained a dying man with nails in his body draped on a cross for all to see and gawk at.

"Don't look at him. You're so touchy," she replied.

"How can I help it? He's right in front of us."

"He resurrected, you know, after they buried him."

"Resurrected?"

"He came to life after he died."

"Like a ghost?"

"No, as a real person. Then he rose to heaven. Don't you know anything? You know Buddhists can't go to heaven," she declared, taking a different direction.

"They do so. We have a place called nirvana."

"That's not a real heaven."

"It is so."

"You're misguided. You have to be Christian to ascend to heaven."

Misguided? Ascend? Such big words. What a show-off! Always Miss Smarty Pants, teacher's pet… "Helen sits so nicely, hands folded. She's always *prepared. Helen is a perfect example. Try to be like her." Secretly, though, I envied her and sometimes tried to imitate her. What did that feel like . . . perfection? Bodhisattva was perfect, but he only sat there not having much fun.*

Perfect or not, though, I defended myself: "I'll ask the reverend next Sunday."

"Every religion has its own version of heaven," the reverend replied to my question.

That was OK. We would each have more space that way.

Now I looked again at the cross in Terry Hall. Would a figure of Christ appear on it? How about a cheerful Christ? Smiling, hopeful. Would Helen say that was blasphemy?

Finally, my turn came to be led home. By now the wind had slackened into bursts. A wind spout carried a funnel of sand over a barrack. Other barracks emerged in the gloom.

"I can make it alone," I said.

"No, hold my hand," Sumi's father insisted.

We walked a block, then I pushed his hand away and ran home.

My mother threw open the door. Sand billowed into the room, but she didn't notice. For a second, she stretched out her arms as if to hug me, but she checked herself and said, "You are back safely," and handed me a bottle of warm orange Nehi.

"Where's this from?" I asked.

"I kept it for a special day. There's one more for Sumiya."

I wiped the bottle and sipped. It reminded me of the after-school snacks my mother had waiting for us in Los Angeles, almost always fresh orange juice and a cookie to "keep us until dinner."

"I wish . . . ," I began.

"No use to wish," she cut me off. "Life is what it is. *Gaman.*"

Temple 7G

From the trunk that my mother had packed in Los Angeles, I retrieved my metronome and my set of *The Scribner Radio Music Library,* each volume lovingly protected with kraft paper. The set, along with my piano lessons and the piano itself, were purchased on the payment plan with money that my mother had put aside, dollar by dollar. I asked her why she had packed them.

"So you can practice," my mother informed me.

"With no piano?" I asked, half sad and half glad at that notion.

"We'll find one."

"We will?"

What was she thinking? I had had two years of lessons but was no model student. I practiced halfheartedly with one eye on the clock—one half hour—and one ear on the laughter and chatter of my friends outside. I was stuck inside with scales, Hanon exercises, and the metronome.

The metronome. *Click. Click. Click. Click.* Mo-no-to-nous. *Tick. Tick. Tick. Tick.* The metal arm tapped on and on. When it ran down, I rewound it with the gold-plated key stuck to its side. Adagio, andante, allegro: funny foreign names just to say slow, medium, fast. Hypnotists put their patients into a trance by swinging a pendulum back and forth, back and forth, back and forth. I could go to sleep. C major scale. Up and down, up and down. C-D-E-F-G-A-B-C. Then C minor: C-D-E flat-F-G-A flat-B-C. *C-tick. D-tick. Sleep-tick.*

"Good pianists keep good time," Miss Wilker had instructed. "Evenly: one, two, three, four. Listen to the beat. Oh, no, Yuriko, Beethoven wouldn't want the *Fur Elise* to sound like a march, would he? Now, softly and le-ga-to—draw it o-u-t—softly—sweetly—si-ng. Yes, sing with it, and you will hear the beauty of the line."

My clunking didn't add any beauty, but when Miss Wilker played the piece, yes, I heard the beauty. Yes, it was beautiful. But for a nine-year-old hand to express that kind of transcendence? I asked her to repeat the piece—I wanted to hear the beautifulness again, but Miss Wilker thought I was dragging my feet. It was my turn. I played, pretending I was Beethoven dedicating these notes to Elise, whoever she was. Miss Wilker said I needed more practice. She always said that.

The truth was that metronome restricted me. I wanted to play freely and express myself the way the advanced students played, their eyes shut, bodies swaying, wrists floating up from the keyboard. Yes, without the incessant ticking I could be expressive.

"Yuriko, please!" Miss Wilker struck her pencil on the side of the piano: *thud, thud.*

Jazz. Someone had told me that when you played jazz, you could make up anything; you could improvise. You could play fast or slow, and nobody cared because you were baring your soul.

"Miss Wilker? Can I play jazz?" I asked her.

"Of course, dear, someday, when you play better, but right now, please listen to the metronome: one, two, three, four. Make the melody sing."

One day, as my mother had predicted, two out-of-tune upright pianos miraculously appeared at Amache. One found a home in the auditorium of the new high school; the other, oddly, in a barrack of Block 8K, close enough so I could practice every few days. Miss Mary Watanabe, a Nisei pianist, offered lessons.

One day I showed Miss Watanabe a Scribner volume. "The dust will ruin it. Put it away," she directed, probably understanding its value, both in money and uniqueness in camp.

"Why doesn't she want to use them? I brought them all the way from Los Angeles for you," my mother asked.

"She said they were 'too precious.'"

"Tell her I want you to use them," my mother insisted.

I didn't want to mediate between them. I wrapped the books in newspaper and placed them under my bed. My mother made no further comment about them.

Piano practice in Amache was a challenge and was interrupted by more than windstorms. At one afternoon session, I heard tapping on the window. Three friends—Eva, Tami, and Katy—peeked in. I smiled. *Tic, tic, tic:* they continued pecking. I glanced up. Tami began to strike the glass with a rock.

I cried out, "Stop that!" and doggedly finished my scales. Eva began to sing off-key: "Mary had a little lamb, little lamb..." Tami and Katy pounded on the wall.

It was useless. My practice was spoiled. When I stepped outside, they scurried away like mice.

At dinner the three of them ignored me. I sat alone, humiliated and puzzled. I was sure everyone was staring at me.

Later that evening I wondered aloud why people were so mean sometimes. My mother consoled me. "Mostly to feel bigger than everyone."

My three friends—friends?—ignored me for a week, and then suddenly, we were buddies again, and they suggested a Monopoly game. I told them I had a new Nancy Drew book I wanted to read.

"Have it your way," Eva said. I found myself on the outs again for a week.

We all seemed bound by Eva's whims. One week it was Katy's, then Tami's turn to be rejected. I hated authoritarian figures, but even more than that, I feared being erased, shunned like a leper, so I went along with Eva. The drama played on for another year into the sixth grade until one day— like a bolt from the blue—I realized that there were other girls in camp who could be my friends; there were other acts to follow. When I refused to be intimidated, Eva's power play fizzled.

It was not until I was much older in college that I understood that this kind of activity was part of a twelve- and thirteen-year-old's rite of passage. Not many girls escape being pulled into the game, and most of us remember it as an agonizing period in our lives.

My father, meanwhile, found fellow idlers in the rec room. They played poker or mahjong or sat around contemplating the lists of outside jobs in the East posted on the bulletin board: "Chick sexers needed; room and board plus good wages. Will train." "Chauffeur for well-to-do family. Will provide transportation from center." "Work on modern farm. All amenities provided." "Service personnel for deluxe hotel. Live in comfort in one of our rooms." The war had depleted the male workforce, and in desperation employers were turning to manpower in the camps.

"You could get a job in the mess hall," my mother suggested.

"That's all you think I'm good for?"

"You have experience as a cook."

"I can make more money outside."

What kind of life would I have had with a different father? One like Helen's maybe. I'd be greeted with hugs and smiles. Well, maybe not hugs because Japanese dads didn't do that, but anyway he would have smiled and brought me little surprise trinkets. Perhaps, though, an ideal father was a myth. I heard about them at Sunday school and grade school. *Life* magazine had ads for washing machines with pictures of a beaming family gathered around sparkling white sheets and towels—was this the happy family with the father providing the means for clean clothes?

No, my perfect father would be one who shared a day on a merry-go-round, who took me fishing and camping, who taught me how to change a tire, who laughed at my jokes and praised me when I learned something new like shooting a bow and arrow. He'd do crossword puzzles with me and help me with my spelling. He'd read me stories at bedtime and tell me he loved me.

But, sadly, that kind of love was not something my father had ever experienced himself…so he didn't know how to express it. He'd been abandoned. How could I expect him to act that way? Now it was too late, way too late.

Sometime before Thanksgiving that first year in camp, my father left us, joining a group of men leaving for Seabrook Farms in New Jersey. "Mind your mother," he said. He relinquished what mythical power he had as he once again moved away from me. Carrying his checkered cardboard suitcase, he boarded the back of a panel truck, blending with the men who all wore hats, white shirts, and ties. They looked like apprehensive schoolboys as they jostled for standing space. He had no idea how long he would be gone, but he said that he would send money back.

My mother and I stood by the entrance gate and waved until the truck disappeared down the dirt road. I was losing my father all over again.

•

There were two Buddhist "temples" at Blocks 7G and 12G. My mother and I attended services at the closer one at 7G. For the first few months, a table with a bowl of incense sticks served as the altar. I remembered the Los Angeles temple where incense smoke had engulfed me as soon as I stepped into the hall. A shimmering gold Buddha dominated the front. We bowed in *gassho*. My mother told me that the beads on the long rosary twisting from the priest's hand had been carved from the holy Bodhi Tree. Beneath its branches, Buddha had meditated for years until he attained enlightenment in a burst of light.

Had he shattered? Did his body pieces sprinkle down and clump into this solid statue? Did the earth melt golden, hardening into this massive meditative form with its spectators stunned speechless? No, that's not the way it happened. He retained his human form and set off, like Jesus, to preach his gospel throughout India. "Life is suffering," he said. People agreed, "Yes, we suffer. Deliver us from our suffering," they cried. "Yes, I can do that," he preached. "Follow the Noble Eightfold Path with me." And they did. By the hundreds, they followed.

One Sunday after the service, I stood close to the priest and touched his rosary, hoping for a magical day, but it turned out to be just like any other day. I went home, changed into my everyday clothes, ate my lunch, and spent the afternoon playing with my friends. So much for miracles.

One Sunday in Amache, a golden altar replaced the table. It housed an elongated Buddha carved from scrap wood by a resident. Gratefully, the priest performed a dedication ceremony. Waving a wand capped with red and white streamers, he chanted a solemn sutra, sucking in his breath loudly as if the effort was too great for mortal man. My mother closed her eyes and softly chanted in unison with the priest.

"You knew that sutra?" I asked, incredulous, after the service.

"It's the same one as in Japan. I listened to my Honorable Father."

"And memorized it?"

"He was a Zen priest. I loved the peace inside the temple. So quiet. I helped my father even though it was my brother's job. He'd rather play outside, so I took his job: cleaned the altar, watered the flowers, emptied the incense pots. I listened to every sutra and memorized them. I even learned when to strike the bell. *Ding…ding.* Such a clear, strong sound. Father said prayers at my mother's shrine after dinner. We prayed for her soul in nirvana and lit a candle so her path to heaven would be bright. We offered flowers so she had something sweet to smell and see on her journey.

The Block 7G Buddhist Church girls' group.

"Now I pray every night for her and father and sister. I hope they are content. After I die, I will be content if you pray for me and include my mother and father and sister every day."

"I didn't even know them, Mom," I said.

"Never mind, then. I will pray from my grave. Too much to ask…a simple prayer."

How had this conversation gotten so twisted? I felt guilty and manipulated, but how could I refuse? "Well…um…OK, Mom. I'll offer prayers for the three of you. And Dad, too. Does it have to be in Japanese?"

"They don't understand English."

"I'll try. You'll have to teach me a prayer in Japanese."

"Yes, it's enough to try," she said, pleased.

We left our discussion hanging. My mother never brought up the subject again.

•

Before the war, we had celebrated Christmas, even though we were Buddhists. We exchanged simple gifts and shopped for a tree. One of my mother's dressmaking clients gave us a special Santa Claus ornament. "Be careful with that," she cautioned. "It was hand-blown in Germany. It's valuable." Why would she entrust us with an item of such value?

My brother and I added paper ornaments we made at school—the gold and silver Japanese lanterns fashioned by folding and slitting a paper cylinder. My brother straightened the previous year's tinfoil icicles and hung them, one by one, on the branches. If I impatiently flung a handful, he took them off and rehung them: "That's wrong. They look messy," he complained. I quit and let him finish.

One year Uncle Tamaki, my father's friend, visited. He produced a shiny nickel and a dirty dime on his palm and asked us to pick one.

I pointed at the bigger nickel.

My brother took the dime. "Ha," he said, "a dime is worth two of your nickels."

I vowed that the next year I wouldn't be fooled again. I hated Tamaki-san for tricking me. It made me feel so stupid.

"Oh, yes," he said. "Here are special big socks you can hang up for Santa. Merry Christmas." Mr. Tamaki beamed. He was a Buster Brown socks salesman.

"We don't have a fireplace," I reminded him. Besides, Santa Claus didn't visit us. There was no reason to hang the socks. We saved them to grow into.

But we remembered our manners. "Thank you very much, Uncle Tamaki," we said.

Another special holiday treat was a trip to the May Company window displays. Plaster carolers, mouths gaping, sang to music crackling from loudspeakers. Mary cradled Jesus like a jewel. Turbaned wise men bore gifts. A cardboard village surrounded the trunk of a huge tree spangled with glass globes. Santa Claus and his elves moved stiffly side to side, hammering on the same toy. Tiny ceramic children sledded on a cotton-batting hill sprinkled with glitter.

I begged to go inside. "Next year. We have to go now," my mother tugged me away. In another window, I glimpsed a princess doll—blond curls showering down her back—wrapped in a shimmering pink gown dotted with pearls and sequins. She took my breath away. "That's what I want for Christmas," I told my mother as we hurried away.

•

When Pearl Harbor was bombed, rumors flew: all the Japanese would be forced back to Japan. We were the enemy. Immobilized by fear, we stopped attending church and prayed at home in front of a benign Buddha painted on a scroll: "I want to stay in America. I don't even speak Japanese—well, not much. We celebrate Christmas every year so that makes us Americans. Oh, please. *Namu amida butsu.*"

We skipped presents and a tree that year. I didn't get the princess doll.

The following year in 1942 at Amache, Christmas unfolded in tantalizing bits. Our priest tacked celluloid holly above the windows. Some barrack windows framed a candle. A few people found stunted skeletal trees or bushes and decorated them. An artist offered a silk-screening class for printing Christmas cards. Mrs. Bender introduced carols in class. When we had memorized a half dozen, we joined the other fifth-grade class and wandered through neighboring barracks.

"Smile, children, smile," Mrs. Bender advised. "Sing with gladness."

I had never gone "a-caroling"—it was not a California tradition. I was freezing. My toes and fingers felt like icicles. My lips wouldn't open. Gladness was definitely not what I felt. A few people peered curiously from their windows; no one braved the cold to come outside.

"Smile. Open your mouths wide," Mrs. Bender encouraged. "There's hot cocoa waiting back at the school."

Hot cocoa! That woke me from my reluctance. I sang with vigor, and what a delicious treat that was—real cocoa with a cookie!

At the final church service of the year, the reverend reminded us that Christ, Buddha, and Muhammad were all great saviors: "They envisioned a world of love and compassion. Buddha taught that salvation was achieved through a pure heart and rightful intentions. Christ sacrificed himself to save mankind. Buddha renounced a princely life and meditated for years

A silk-screening class was offered in camp. This Christmas card, given to my mother in 1942, is an example of the creative work that the students produced.

to attain salvation. Muhammad taught from a holy book called the Koran. Whatever your beliefs, the key word is 'love.' *Namu amida butsu.*"

"Merry Christmas," he announced. "I hope to see you after Oshougatsu; Happy New Year!"

Holiday packages arrived. My parents received a card from Mr. and Mrs. Harrington. My mother pressed the envelope to her breast for a second—a fleeting prayer—before she slit the edge with her nail file. Only a signature, not a message, identified the card, but folded within was a check—a check for ten dollars, one week's pay before the war.

She carefully tucked the check into her purse. No one had ever offered my parents "free" money. Money had to be earned. Perhaps Mrs. Harrington was keeping her promise of the ruby glasses. Perhaps one day that

The Block 6H mess hall, probably during the Christmas season. Our Block 9L mess hall was draped with green and red crepe paper in a similar manner. (Photo gift of Jack Muro, Japanese American National Museum, 2012.2.317; reprinted by permission of the Japanese American National Museum. Copyright 2013. All rights reserved.)

seed money would enable us to find a way to those gleaming goblets traced with gold.

On Christmas Eve, we anticipated a special dinner. I hurried into the mess hall even before the cook rang the mess bell, as did everyone else. I stopped short inside the door. A startling transformation had taken place. Floating through the hall was Bing Crosby's creamy voice crooning "White Christmas." Green and red crepe paper twisted across the ceiling. Candles flickered on some tables. A scrawny tree glistened with pine cones, yarn balls, funny-paper cranes, and newspaper chains. Most wondrous of all, an angel crowned the glittering tree—a quiet, serene one with her eyes closed. Someone had tenderly pleated her cellophane wings, which fluttered imperceptibly, catching slivers of light.

Suddenly Santa Claus burst in. What a strange sight! He wore a mask with upside-down, crescent-moon eyes, a cotton-batting beard, and sagging red pajamas. It didn't matter, though, because packages cascaded from two laundry bags. Although the packages read "adult male or woman," "child boy or girl," he knew our names and dispersed the gifts with "ho, ho, ho! Merry Christmas, Mrs. Sumida. Merry Christmas, Tommy."

When a mother restrained a toddler from wading into the pile with "no, no, we must wait," the baby burst into tears, inciting a chorus of more wails. "Here, here" Santa said. He grabbed some random packages and tossed them to the children. In his haste, he handed me one labeled "child boy." I unwrapped a wooden yo-yo.

"You got a yo-yo; what a yo-yo you are!" a boy teased. "Santa thinks you're a boy. You're a boy."

"Girls can play with yo-yos, too. See, I can make it spin," I bragged. I flipped the toy down, but it didn't return. I tried again.

"Boys are better at that," he boasted.

I flung the yo-yo toward him: "Here, you can have it then." I tried to sound flippant. I wanted desperately to master this simple toy, but I hated being butterfingered in front of all the other kids.

My mother rescued me. "Let's have dinner together tonight," she said and led the way into the mess line. I filled my tray with ham and cranberry sauce and sat next to her at the long table.

My mother touched my arm. "Look," she said. She placed a yo-yo between us.

"I know I can learn to do tricks with this," I said.

"Yes, I know," my mother answered.

That night the barbed wire and guard towers with the pacing soldiers were like remote dreams. The soldiers maybe even envied us—inside by the warmth of a coal stove and wishing each other a better New Year.

I was happy.

3

Seasons, Joys, and Sorrows

OKASANE

The Amache winds! How do I describe them? They blew and howled, they choked and caressed, but Eva's mother had one especially colorful description: "Tit and butt busters."

"Look at those tits and butts," she'd say as she stared at the women bracing themselves against the wild wind. "Huge…bounce like water balloons." Eva's mother was the strangest person I'd ever met. She repelled and fascinated me. Skeletal and pale, she wore cherry-colored lipstick, defined by black edges. She looked like a woman who'd say "butt." She spit out the word, curling her lips around the sound, daring anyone within earshot to protest.

Oshiri, revered bottom, was my mother's hushed term for buttocks. "Wipe oshiri cleanly. Use only a little paper…don't waste," she warned me as a child. "Don't wiggle." But here was a woman hailing this body part as if she were announcing a fashion show: "Yes, ladies, watch closely…here she comes…hmmm…too flat front and back." Embarrassed, beet red, the woman with the unassuming behind hurried away. Eva and her mother guffawed. I tried to laugh but managed only a grin. I was grateful they lived in the next block of barracks. I only knew them because Eva was a classmate.

"You know why you ladies need big behinds?" Eva's mother asked. "Because then the men will lust after you. They like big ones, you know. Good lay."

I waited for her to continue. I knew "to lay" had something to do with sex. Mrs. Bender had explained present, past, and past-perfect tenses: lie, lay, lain. We had recited after her: "I lie down today, I lay down yesterday, I had lain down the day before." I didn't have the courage to ask either woman the connection between the two words.

So there we stood against the door of the laundry room entrance of the neighboring block in tit-busting winds and waited for women to stagger by. Eva's mother commented relentlessly until she wearied of the game and—without a word—ducked through the door, slamming it in our faces. The mystery of sex appeared to present itself only in bits and pieces.

·

The first fall in camp my mother knit four pink rectangles about eight inches long and two inches wide. When I asked about them, she quickly slipped them into a cardboard box. When she left the room, I peeked. Next to the rectangles lay a box labeled Kotex with a picture of a rectangular white pad the same size and shape as the pink ones. Later, I asked her what Kotex was, and she said, hesitantly, that the pads were for blowing noses.

My friend Sachiko, two years older and wiser than I, tittered nervously when I asked if that was true. I asked Eva and Tami, and Eva said she'd ask her mother, who "knew everything." Her mother wore slinky satin nightgowns and devoured detective and romance magazines, then hid them under the mattress. We found the magazines and stared at the lurid photographs of contorted dead bodies.

"I saw a dead body once," I bragged. Eva called me a liar.

It was true. Helen and I had been playing outside her Los Angeles home when we heard a thud like a weighty package thrown onto the lawn next door. Curious, we walked over. A woman sprawled face down like a puppet. Blood oozed from her stomach, flushing bright red. My own blood drained into my toes. My arms prickled.

We stood rooted until someone inside the house called, *"Oi, omae,* darling, are you OK?" A man, clad in pajamas, peeked out the door. Then, spying the body, he screamed at us and fled into the street, yelling, "Call the police! Somebody call the police!" The man pushed us away: "You kids, scram." My legs wouldn't move. I had seen this woman only yesterday, flipping her hair from her face as she strode down the street. Now she was dead.

"Wow," Eva remarked, "that's cool."

Her mother walked in, grabbed the magazines, and cried, "That's the kind of junk your father reads." She tossed them into a wastebasket. *Who was she kidding?*

Eva shrugged her shoulders and asked her mother about Kotex. Her mother rolled her eyes and said, "It's part of 'the curse.'"

"The curse?" Eva repeated.

"Women are cursed with blood from their body every month," her mother keened dramatically. She touched the back of her hand to her forehead and moaned, "Oh, alas, we are cursed."

This lady is crazy, I thought. I backed away as fast as I could.

A few weeks later at recess, Amy refused to play and pressed her back against the coal bin. I touched her arm, and she burst into tears. When Mrs. Bender coaxed her away from the bin, a bloody blotch marked the spot where she had been leaning. We moved away, frightened.

"It's all right, children. Girls, come inside. I'll explain," Mrs. Bender told us.

We learned about menstruation and the way a baby grows inside the mother for nine months. The Kotex mystery was solved. Mrs. Bender exhibited a sample. "This will be in my drawer for emergencies," she said. "You don't need to be ashamed. It's a natural phenomenon."

Someone asked the "big question": "How does the baby get inside the mother?"

Mrs. Bender babbled about "seeds planted" and "eggs developing," but none of us could follow her explanation.

I asked, "How does the baby come out? Through the navel?"

"Oh, no. There's a special place between the legs."

We compared notes after school: "You get a baby by kissing." "No, you have to French kiss." "I think the man's, you know, 'thing' has something to do with it." "Yeah, but what?" "That's where the seeds are."

Seeds? We knew what seeds were—we found them inside apples, oranges, pomegranates, even cucumbers and tomatoes. The penis was shaped like a cucumber. I visualized neat rows of seeds planted inside, waiting to sprout into tiny babies. Did they get watered whenever the man peed?

The pink pads remained a puzzle until one day I "started." I ran to my mother and announced, "I've got my period. I need a Kotex pad."

"Who told you about that?"

"Mrs. Bender."

"In school? The Japanese never talk about such things."

She pulled out a pad—the pink rectangle—and an elastic belt with two tabs. She showed me how to place the pad on the rectangle and fasten the rectangle to the tabs with safety pins, front and back. It was a pad holder!

I asked her how she had found out about periods if nobody talked about them.

"I thought I was sick, so I put some leaves and cloth between my legs, but the blood didn't stop. I was afraid to tell father. I thought I might die. I went to the herbalist lady, who gave me a cloth, like a diaper, and told me to use it to soak the blood and wash it every night. She told my father I was ready."

"Ready?"

"To have babies."

"Um, Mom, Mrs. Bender didn't tell us exactly how babies happen."

"When you marry, your husband will tell you." My mother evaded the question.

"He will?"

Then I made another discovery. I was allergic to woolen pink pads.

"I can't stand this; it itches like crazy," I complained.

"It feels funny at first, but it will be better soon," my mother assured me.

But it wasn't. I pulled up my skirt and showed her the rash lacing my thighs.

She gasped, then ripped apart a cotton pillowcase and sewed new holders.

I offered the pink pads to Tami and Eva. They took them, pinching their faces as if I were offering poison. I don't think they ever used them, though.

•

Sometimes I thought it was just as well that cameras were forbidden in camp because, if there was such a thing as an awkward age, then I was certainly in it. One day I was on my way to school.

"Hey, Four Eyes," Tommy called out.

"Not again," I thought. "Not another LeRoy."

"Four Eyes, Four Eyes, face like an apple pie," he chanted.

I kept walking. This latest pestering had begun with Health Day. A visiting nurse arrived to measure our blood pressure and to check our scalps and toes. We read from an eye chart, and I found the bottom half blurred. I could see only the top three lines.

My mother and I visited Dr. Fuji at the dispensary. After a short exam, he pulled out a tray of eyeglass frames. I chose a red pair with rhinestones despite my mother's protest that they were too bright.

"The others are old-lady glasses. I want these," I insisted.

Dr. Fuji pulled down my eyelid. "Hmmm, there's some unusual redness," he said. "It's a little infection. There's a new medicine called penicillin that will cure everything. Let's try that. You don't want to go blind, do you?"

"No!" I exclaimed.

He handed me a bottle of pink drops. In those maiden days of penicillin, no one knew to refrigerate the medicine. I kept the bottle on the window sill, exposed to sun and dust. I even used it when little green specks turned it into a tealike brew. Dr. Fuji had told me to use up the bottle, so I didn't waste a drop. Years later, I learned from similar symptoms that the redness had been caused by an allergic reaction, not an infection. The miracle penicillin had been useless to me.

When Tommy dared taunt me again, I stared him down until he turned away. I knew I looked cool in my sparkling red glasses.

•

ONLY MY FREEDOM, WATERCOLOR, 30 BY 22 INCHES.
Jackrabbits (painted white here, instead of dirty brown) hopped freely, unfazed by barbed wire
and armed guards. We, however, were confined, trapped. I often saw these animals
when I walked along the fence and envied them.

Winter in California had been a gentle continuation of fall. I wore a jacket when mornings turned crisp and donned boots when it rained. I splashed into the iridescent puddles shimmering at the entrance of the bus maintenance shed on the way to school. I jumped into those green and purple puddles. The colors fractured into stars: red, gold, blue. I hopped into another little lake. Tiny rainbows swirled insanely like drunken bugs. Raindrops pocked the oily surface, then bounced off as flecks of light. I squatted and smeared the edge of a puddle oozing with tarry liquid. My finger smelled of dirt and gas.

Winter in Amache was sometimes gentle, often brutal, but always amazing. The first winter began with a chill suspended in the air. The sky was gray and featureless…a studied watercolor wash. A few small snowflakes flitted in midair, dancing as if unable to make up their minds, then floated to the ground. The flakes, weightless, melted instantly on my palm. I glimpsed a fleeting crystal on the back of my hand. The flakes wavered before they touched the ground and disappeared. As I stood there, they fell faster, clung to my clothes, and feathered the sagebrush.

Soon the snow fell in clusters. I went inside and watched snow temper the angles of the barracks and glaze the windows. A gentle wind sculpted the snow into soft mounds. The desert was transformed into wispy cotton candy, swollen *mochi,* bloated meringues. The monotonous gray was layered with a soft sheen muted by the golden reflections of a late-afternoon sun trying bravely to push aside the clouds.

I whipped at the snow with my feet to the end of our block and looked toward the vastness of Kansas, smothered by the same white blanket. Jackrabbits hopped through the barbed-wire fence, oblivious to the armed guards, nibbling at the scraps the mess cook had left for them. I crept closer and tried to coax one near. For a second, it looked at me, then scampered away. "Come on," it seemed to say, "follow me." I watched as it tracked black prints in the snow.

"I envy you, Mr. Rabbit," I told him. "You're free. You can hop to Kansas if you want." I yearned for this place I had never seen and barely knew about, but it lay beyond the barbed wire, beyond the reaches of the searchlights. It symbolized nirvana, the Promised Land.

That glimpse of Kansas heaven had to wait almost sixty years before it became real. In 1998 there was an Amache camp reunion. My son and I went two days before the official celebration to visit the camp. In our rental car, we stopped at the entrance, where a faded wooden sign pointed to the road where so many years earlier I had bid my father good-bye.

"I used to stand by the barbed-wire fence and wish I could squeeze through like the rabbits and make my way to Kansas," I told Michael.

"The state line is only about fifteen miles away," he said and turned the car around.

We drove away from Amache and soon spied a sign displaying a huge sunflower. "Welcome to Kansas," it beckoned. I stepped out on the side of the road.

"You've been to Kansas now," Michael said.

What could I reply? "Thank you" wasn't enough.

◆

With the onset of winter, we ordered sturdier clothes. From the Monkey Ward catalog, I chose a dark green wool suit—pants and a jacket sporting a hood fastened by a pom-pom drawstring. A hood! So mysterious and glamorous. Movie stars swathed themselves in velvet capes with hoods.

We tore open the package when it arrived. The snowsuit was a garish bottle green, and the wool matted like felt. The hood clung to my skull like a bandage. However, I loved the pom-poms, that is, until they became wet and clumped into tight golf balls. Then I cut them off.

"Wartime," my mother consoled. "They use the good wool for the soldiers. Anyway this is warmer than a sweater."

Yes, it was warm at first but hardly water resistant. By the time I slushed through the snow to school, my pants were sopping wet. I draped them by the potbellied stove with other pants and jackets, where they steamed dry. The cloying odor was nauseating. I moved near a window to breathe the wisps of air that blew in.

My mother didn't order a coat for herself. When it stormed, she bundled up in her old coat and a raincoat that someone had given her. She tied a woolen kerchief around her head.

"Let's order a new coat, Mom," I said each time she donned this ragtag outfit. "You don't want to look like a beggar," I teased her with her own admonition, remembering her insistence that we should wear our good clothes on that fateful day when we had registered for our trip to Santa Anita. We received a small clothing allowance from the government. Why was she reluctant to use it?

"This is enough. Father had only straw sandals to wear, summer and winter. I wish I had sent him shoes when he was alive."

"So by freezing, you're trying to make things up somehow to your father?" I asked. "That was a long, long time ago."

"I want to feel snow the way he did. Poor father. Only one pair of sandals. One time he carried me *onbu*, piggyback, to school because the snow was so deep. He wrapped his feet in cloth before we went, but they were soaking wet even before we reached the road. This was a special day to present the teacher with a New Year's treat—incense to clean the air of unwanted spirits—so I had to go."

•

Before the war, New Year's festivities had played a primary role in the Japanese community. In camp its significance was manifested by traditional *mochi tsuki,* rice-cake pounding. Camp or no camp, this was an important event. Some enterprising craftsmen found a large tree stump, chiseled a shallow bowl in one end, and set it outside the mess hall. Women dumped hot glutinous rice into the cavity. Two men began pounding it with huge wooden mallets.

Pettanko, uuh, pettanko. Thump, uuh, thump. Thump, uuh, thump.

A woman stood ready to turn and fold the rice between strikes.

"Ya!"

Pettanko, uuh, pettanko.

"Ya!"

Plumes of steam curled above the rice mixture. Our breaths feathered around us. Sweat soaked the *hachimaki,* the scarf wrapped around the men's brows.

"Hey, aim straight," yelled one man. "You don't want mashed hands."

"Don't worry," the man with the mallet answered. "As long as I keep my eye on the hair around the hole, I won't miss."

All the men roared. The women giggled. *What was so funny?* I wondered.

The woman kneaded the mochi without missing a beat, her hands red from the heat. After ten minutes, she nodded to another woman who was standing ready by her side, and then smoothly—as if rehearsed—the second woman stepped into the first one's space and continued to turn the sticky mass.

Pettanko, uuh, pettanko. Thump, uuh, thump.

The rhythm was hypnotic. Someone began beating a block of wood with sticks: "Ya!" *thunk, thunk,* "Ya!" *thunk, thunk.* Some men, slightly drunk, hopped about in a dance.

In Los Angeles, we bought ready-made mochi. My mother dropped them into a special soup, *ozoni,* for New Year's breakfast. I savored this hot broth with bits of dried seaweed, tofu, and green onion.

"Yes, eat, eat," my mother urged. "Mochi will start the New Year with a pure heart and good luck. A new beginning." Sometimes we toasted some mochi on top of the range on an asbestos pad until they popped and the innards oozed like marshmallows. We dipped them in savory mixtures—soy sauce and sugar, roasted soybean flour, red bean paste—and ate them with gusto.

We bought two special flat mochi for *okasane* that we placed in front of our altar to bless our ancestors. We placed a Satsuma tangerine with one or two leaves atop this stack of mochi. This tower squatted there until the cakes dried into cement and green mold blossomed between the mochi and then spread like measles onto the white surfaces. My mother lit a candle and some incense sticks each morning and prayed, sometimes silently but more often in a murmuring drone. "There," she'd say, "they will rest in peace. They will be content."

•

At Amache the mochi paste was dumped onto a mess table, where the women pinched off a portion and rolled it into a small ball. The balls were left to cool and harden, but somehow they seemed to disappear almost as soon as they were set down, especially when someone added a dab of red bean paste on top. My friends and I snitched one or two. The women playfully slapped our hands but didn't restrain us. Everyone was too happy to scold. When at last the dumplings were made, the women—flushed red with the exertion—shed their aprons and contemplated their work with a sigh: "Ah, good job."

•

Winter nights at Amache tested our endurance, our bodies, and our spirits. We banked the coals in the stove, placed a kettle of water on top, and checked for glowing embers on the floor before retiring. Snuggled under the bedding, I bicycled my frigid toes until they were warm.

Amache at night. Photo courtesy of Gary Ono.

NIGHTMARE, WATERCOLOR, 22 BY 30 INCHES.
Coyotes were abundant and roamed at night, wailing. Sometimes I thought I heard them padding beneath my window.

Coyotes began wandering closer to the barracks, perhaps seeking the warmth radiating from the buildings. They padded toward the barracks silently, so silently. During the day, I sometimes spied them fleetingly in the distance like a mirage. Once a pair of pups bounced after their mother, who slunk away beneath the brush. When night fell, their hesitant howls began, a single wail at first, followed by a long silence. Then far off in the distance, an answering call floated in the stillness. As if awakening from a long slumber, others began to signal across the desert with their eerie descending cry. There was such sadness in it; the sound trailed away until another animal responded with the same lamenting wail. Soon they formed a chorus.

One night I thought I heard one scratching beneath my window. A furtive rustle betrayed its presence. I imagined flaming red eyes, bristling fur, a snarling mouth. It was ready to pounce and devour me. I curled into a tight ball and pulled the covers over my head.

Snowstorms blew in from all directions in southeastern Colorado. From Kansas the snow bonded with the dust and sand of the Great Plains and fell heavily, tinged with a tawny hue. The barracks and the desert mutated into darker shades as if God had dipped a giant brush into a paint pot and flung it across the land. Even the sky turned a threatening brown. After successive storms, I could slice a section of snow off our coal bin and find layers—pure white alternating with myriad shades of tan and beige flecked with black coal. Once I presented a dish of small tartlets of stratified snow to my mother. She hesitated a moment, gingerly picked one up, and ate it. She actually ate it! She smiled and claimed the snow tarts were the best dessert she'd ever tasted.

If the storm pushed in from the north, the snow fell crystalline as if to prove that the vastness of Canada, Wyoming, and Montana was pure and virginal. Those storms brought crisp falling temperatures, sometimes hovering around zero for a week at a time. We stuffed paper and strips of cloth around the windows to seal out the cold, but they were useless against the relentless onslaught. We woke to find miniature mounds of snow on the windowsills with tiny icicles dangling below.

I was grateful for the puffy comforter that my mother and I had quilted…a slick Japanese print on top, pale orange on the bottom. On

I posed by the coal bin at Barrack 9C to show off the icicles in 1944.
We finally had access to cameras near the end of the war.

The Block 6H laundry room; ours was identical. (Photo gift of Jack Muro, Japanese American
National Museum, 2012.2.3; reprinted by permission of the Japanese American National
Museum. Copyright 2013. All rights reserved.)

the barrack floor, she had shown me how to measure and tack the fabric together. I had grumbled about all the preliminary steps, but she had confidently ignored the protests. She knew better.

The western winds and snow rarely reached us. The Rockies snagged the brunt of those storms, and by the time they had wasted their fury on the craggy peaks, there was little left for us. Only once do I remember a storm wafting ocean smells with it; my throat tightened with nostalgia.

Southern storms tantalized us in late winter with whiffs of spring. Heavy moist flakes fell with a vengeance for a short time, then stopped abruptly. The sky cleared into faultless blue. A short time later, another flurry of snow dropped; then the sky emerged again in a breathtaking azure.

But no matter the direction of its origin, a snowstorm accompanied by an unchecked wind whipped at us with vengeful fury. It pasted our coats around us. Fragments of sagebrush froze to our clothes. We stumbled about muffled in stiff sheets of snow, so when we found shelter, the layers of icy snow broke apart, and we peeled them off in chunks. The foundations of the barracks disappeared in a slope of snow that sometimes reached our windows. The onslaught eclipsed whole barracks.

•

Washing our hair and doing laundry were huge problems in the winter. I put off washing my hair until my itchy scalp became intolerable. After shampooing I bound my hair with a towel and dashed for home. More than once the towel flew off, and by the time I reached my barrack, my hair was flattened like a bullet. I stood shivering by the potbellied stove and fluffed my hair back into presentable shape.

Coping with laundry was much different from Santa Anita. Drying wet clothes presented a hurdle. We could hang them on the lines crossing the laundry room, but a local black market did a brisk business in bedding and clothes, and the thieves became skillful at slipping away with an item or two. Or we could lug the wet clothes home, drape them on makeshift poles in front of the potbellied stove, and periodically rotate them. If we forgot to turn them, we sometimes found our clothing toasted. Sheets might take days to dry and forget about jeans—the men wore them damp, hoping that body heat would eventually dry them. I discovered that my tolerance for soiled clothes was higher than I had imagined; I didn't need to change what I wore every day. Fewer dirty clothes equaled less laundry.

Kanshaku

Yet the winters revealed unbearable beauty. After an especially vicious storm, the desert astounded me. The ground undulated like ocean waves cresting and dipping to the horizon. It drooped and curved into troughs like corrugated washboards. Icy turrets and spires formed on the brush and stretched upward. Ice shards dazzled with a blinding brilliance. A tiny movement—a rabbit leaping—flashed for a moment, then disappeared. The mounded snow beside the pathways was sculpted into twisted and tortured shapes: a line of modern sculptures. Pathways crunched sharply as I tattooed a line of footprints. Melting snow, unimpeded by insulation, dripped off the roofs steaming in the sun and formed long stalactites, sparkling with all the colors in the world. Twice that first season, they crusted into a roof-to-ground barrier.

To prevent the eaves from being crushed by the weight, we smashed the huge icicles with shovels and brooms. I helped reluctantly at first—the glittering wall was too precious to destroy. But as the icicles crashed to the ground, sending plumes of snow dancing into the air, I swung harder and harder until only stubs were left hanging from the eaves. From the doomed icicles on the ground emerged another miracle—a shimmering Atlantis. Frozen buildings leaned crazily askew: breathtakingly, frigidly beautiful.

One child owned an honest-to-goodness Flexible Flyer sled. We lined up impatiently at the top of the slope near Block 9L for a turn riding it. The woolen mittens my mother had knit itched so much that I pulled them off and flew down bare handed, barely able to steer. By the time I had made two turns, I was shivering, soaked through, and thoroughly miserable, but I wouldn't admit it. Sledding was supposed to be the ultimate winter fun, so

I donned the scratchy mittens again, waited in line, and took another turn. When the sled disappeared two weeks later, everyone sympathized with the child and promised to find it. It never reappeared. I felt sorry for the kid, but I didn't really care if the sled turned up or not. We used pieces of cardboard after that.

We spent much of the winter holed up playing Monopoly and cards and manipulating the Ouija board. I was amazed that the Ouija board triangle could magically spell out words. No matter how hard I tried to steady this eerie device, it slowly glided across the board and picked out a letter or number.

"Who is Eva's boyfriend?" we asked. None of us had boyfriends, so it didn't really matter what name presented itself.

"S-T-E-V-W," it spelled.

Steve? Stew? We didn't know anyone named Steve. Try again.

"S-T-E-W-A-R-T."

"Maybe it's someone I'll meet in the future," Eva said. We knew that she had a crush on James Stewart because she had swooned over him in *The Philadelphia Story,* the film that we had seen at the mess hall. We said it was cool that his name showed up, but I suspected that Eva had somehow made the name appear.

Eventually we became impatient with the pace of this game and abandoned it, but Eva's mother continued to play by herself. Trancelike, she stared at her fingers, willing them to give up secrets. Maybe they were lies. So intent was she that once she missed the evening meal and blamed us. "Why didn't you get me? Now I'll starve to death," she wailed.

Once again—before she could do her anguished act—I backed away and sped out the door.

•

The women (but never Eva's mother) gathered in groups of four or five in each other's rooms and knitted and crocheted while keeping up a steady patter of news and gossip. They also played Hanafuda, a Japanese card

RAGE, WATERCOLOR, 22 BY 30 INCHES.

My mother claimed she had a temper, and I witnessed a number of her outbursts; however, she never lashed out against the camp conditions. In this painting, a monster god is doing just that in the light sparking from a guard tower.

game. These dainty cards were stiff and half the size of American cards. The pictures on them were simple but beautiful: cherry blossoms, peonies, chrysanthemums, maple leaves, rain on willows. My friends and I played by matching cards and symbols, but my mother and her friends played more complicated versions that I never understood. I sat and watched anyway. They slapped the cards on the table with a crisp snap, their fingers flicking at a dizzying pace. And they played penny-ante, the coins pinging against the table.

"Mom," I asked, "isn't that gambling, playing with money?"

"It's only pennies. More fun for us."

"I never saw you play cards before."

"This is the first chance I have to learn. Your daddy used to play in Nihonmachi, but he never taught me. He used to gamble big and sometimes lost all his week's pay. I would get so mad. I have *kanshaku,* a terrible temper, so I would chase him out of the house. Now I am so sorry. Women tell me gambling is a sickness, like his drinking. I thought he was doing it to hurt me. When he comes back to camp, I'll try to help him." *Well, that's a change. Does absence really make the heart grow fonder? Even my mother's? Maybe so.*

I remembered once when my father had taken me to Nihonmachi and gambled. I seldom accompanied him anywhere, so this was a special treat...or so I thought.

My father sat me down on a chair and told me to be quiet and just watch. He was going to play pool for a while. He promised to buy me some *manju* later at the confectionery across the street.

The balls rolled and clicked, then thudded into their pockets. My father gave me an assortment of candies and told me once again to stay in the chair. This was confusing. My mother had a rule: sweets after dinner only. I solved that dilemma by eating one, calling it a snack, and saving the rest for later. My father disappeared into another room.

"Where are you going?" I asked, alarmed, and ran after him.

"Stay there. Hey, Chin, watch my baby for a bit, huh?" he addressed a man at the pool table. Chin, intent on his game, nodded absently without so much as a glance at me.

I sat in the chair, swung my feet, and counted: One, back and forth, two, back and forth…I reached fifteen. How long was he going to be? I hated sitting like a zombie doing nothing. My behind was starting to hurt.

I got up and peeked into the next room. It was dark and scary. Men sat around a table, smoking and holding a fan of cards. Small clay circles—blue, yellow, red—were stacked in piles by glasses filled with brown liquid. Cigarette smoke trailed up and formed a billowing cloud above their heads. In the milky light, the cottony mass moved like ghosts peering down. My father glanced at me, but he didn't chase me away, so I stood in the doorway and watched. I started sneezing from the smoke when suddenly Chin jerked me away and plunked me down into the chair again.

"I need to pee," I said.

"Oh, geez," Chin sighed and called out to my father. "Hey, Kay, your kid needs to go."

"I need to pee now," I said. "I can't wait!"

"Tell her to hold it. I'll be there in a minute," my father called.

"No, now!" I yelled back. "Now, now, now!"

Red faced, tight lipped, my father stepped out of the room and pulled me off the seat in a rough swoop.

The restroom had some small round basins on the floor. "What…?" I began.

"Just stand on top of it. Hurry."

"Like a boy?" Boys had weenies to aim their pee. Girls didn't.

I wet the floor, but my father didn't seem to notice.

After more waiting—was I being punished?—my father finally said he'd had enough. He kept his promise, though, and we crossed the street to Fugetsudo. I picked out some confections—cherry blossom wraps and *ânpan*—and took one home for my mother. I was surprised to find her in bed. "I have a bad cold," she explained. She accepted the sweet bun and looked accusingly at my father. He grunted and said he'd make dinner that night. It was a surprisingly good chow mein with crispy fried noodles…better than anything my mother usually made.

•

My father possessed an ivory and bamboo mahjong set. He hid it, so I saw it in his possession only two or three times before the war. I was not allowed to touch it. My mother told me his uncle had given the set to him as a farewell gift. For the few months he lived in camp with us, he shared his set with the other men in the rec room. He refused to teach me how to play—it was "not for kids," he claimed—so when the men were too engrossed to notice me, I sneaked in, sat at the end of the table, and watched. The tiles clinked as the men pushed them into geometric patterns on the table. There were *kanji,* Japanese ideographs, on half of the pieces. I remember the word "*naka*" because that was the first character of our name, Nakai. Naka and *i*—inside of a well.

"Did your family live inside a well?" I teased.

"Of course not. Stop asking stupid questions," my father clipped.

Some tiles had dots; others had flowers or spool-like lines. The confusion of symbols bewildered me. No wonder my father said the game wasn't for kids. When he plunked down a tile and declared victory, I was secretly so proud. Could he see that in my face? He scooped a pile of nickels into a small drawstring bag, pushed one coin toward me, and said, "Don't tell Mama." I didn't, but in this camp, how could she not know?

My father owned few belongings, and I coveted this mahjong set with all my heart. I understood how precious it was to him.

One day I asked, "Daddy, when I'm older will you promise to teach me how to play the game? Maybe, just maybe, can I even have the set?"

"OK, someday," he replied.

I never saw the set again after we left Amache. Maybe it settled a gambling debt.

◆

My mother had diversions, too, not the least of which was her contact with other women, which clearly buoyed her spirits. Along with her teaching position and daily women's circles, she began taking an interest in other religions, local government, and geography. She accompanied friends to Protestant church services and those of other Buddhist sects—Seicho-no-Iye and Nichiren—and found there were four Protestant services each Sunday but only two Buddhist ones. Both sects were Jōdo Shinshū, Pure Land. My mother was a Zen Buddhist but apparently felt no great allegiance to that religious tradition and was free to experience other services.

"Maybe Christians are more faithful," she mused.

"No," I answered. "Helen told me that Protestant means any Christian church outside the Catholic Church, like Methodists, Lutherans, and Presbyterians. She said the Protestants are heathens, and so are the Buddhists."

"Helen is so bright. She knows so much. You should…"

"I know, I know," I cut her off. "I ought to be more like her. You've told me a hundred times."

After her visit to the Nichiren Church, my mother began murmuring the mantra: *"Namu myoho renge kyo, namu myoho renge kyo."* "I devote myself to the Lotus Sutra of the Mystic Law."

After the second day, I asked her please to repeat it to herself: "It's getting on my nerves."

"My friend said to say it out loud so the words will vibrate the air and my Buddhist nature will flower."

"Come again?"

"The words will make the air move so the universe can change."

"It will? Just like that?"

"Every movement influences the air around us. All Buddhists think the same way…everything has a spirit, so we must be careful of what we say, how we act on spirits…spirits of people, of the world. Nichirens think 'namu myoho renge kyo' are very sacred words."

"Whatever," I flippantly answered. "But they still get on my nerves."

She promised to repeat them when she was alone. If I came upon her in midprayer, she whispered the words.

The Seicho-no-Iye service was another one my mother visited. Its doctrine of "natural medicine"—the body could heal itself with no intervention from doctors or drugs—interested her. If one had enough faith in God or Buddha and lived in harmony with nature, then a person would never become seriously ill. Part of the service consisted of testimonials from people who had experienced or heard of healing miracles. For some reason my mother didn't understand, two FBI agents had broken up one of the meetings and written down the names of the participants. The intrusion frightened her, and she stopped attending the services.

And she discovered a new love—geography: exotic lands that she hoped to visit, fantastic people she wanted to meet. She found a tattered world atlas among donated books and perused it, page by page. When Mrs. Bender assigned us all the state capitals to memorize, my mother learned them with me. We were both surprised that the capital of California was not Los Angeles but Sacramento, a farming community in the middle of the state, and that Albany, not New York City, was the capital of New York. We chanted, "Topeka, Cheyenne, Pierre and Providence, Concord and Tallahassee," and tried to trip each other up by repeating them faster and faster.

"One day let's visit all the state capitals," my mother said.

"Yes, we'll circle the whole United States," I replied.

Indeed, my mother traveled in her middle age to foreign lands—Macau, Peru, France and Spain, England and the Netherlands. She saw her brothers and their families in Japan and then extended her Asian excursion to include China, Taiwan, Malaysia, and the Philippines. "But not Africa," she told me, "not Africa. I'm scared of black people."

We talked about our road trip across America once in a while. When at last I found the time—my two sons were grown, my stained glass business could wait—I broached the subject. I wanted to make it real.

"All right, let's do it, Mom. Let's take the summer and drive around all the states. We'll hit all the state capitals."

My mother hesitated, then quietly, very quietly, replied, "No, I'm too tired. I'm too old now."

So—like our trip to the Hollywoodland sign—this one, too, became only a wishful memory.

Obah-San

One day just after New Year's Day, my mother asked me to accompany her to visit my *obah-san,* Grandmother Nakai, who had had a stroke and was in the camp hospital. I was startled. My grandparents' existence in camp had hardly registered with me. I hadn't visited them once in Santa Anita, nor so far in Amache. I knew their address—two blocks north of us—but that was all. My grandmother was a tiny lady with a chirpy baby-bird voice. When my grandparents had farmed in San Juan Capistrano, we had visited them several times, but my only memory was being chased from their house for making too much noise and running into the furrowed fields. My shoes stuck in the soft soil, and I fell, scraping my knees. I was scared to return to the house, so I sat whimpering in the dirt until my mother came looking for me and consoled me.

When my grandparents moved to Los Angeles, my grandmother made it clear that she was not interested in me: "Not tend babies. Babies make me nervous," she told my mother. She was always indifferent and seldom initiated a conversation with me. The one positive memory I have is that single incident when she commented on my energetic dancing performance when I desperately tried to please her. Even then she made only a single terse statement devoid of much feeling. But I do remember a semblance of a tiny, tiny smile.

So now in the middle of the desert, I asked, "Do I have to go with you?"

"Yes," she said. "If she…" My mother stopped, but I knew what she was going to say: "If she dies, you'll be sorry you didn't go to see her. People, um, people can go to heaven so suddenly."

Then she motioned me to sit down. Soberly she related the story of her own mother's unexpected death in Japan. She told me that one night she woke with a start to hear her mother moaning. She stumbled to her mother's side and felt her cheek. It was burning. Alarmed, my mother cried out and roused her father so he might fetch the village doctor. However, he hesitated because it was the middle of the night—he didn't want to disturb the doctor. People contracted fevers, rashes, and coughs every day, and they eventually healed themselves. Finally, at daybreak her father set off, but by the time he and the doctor returned, her mother was dead.

"I should have gone for the doctor myself. I should have gone. It's my fault. Every day I ask Buddha to forgive me," my mother confessed, grief-stricken by the memory.

She continued with her story. "I couldn't believe my mother was gone. One minute she is burning; the next minute she is cold. I begged her to wake up. But she just slept, just slept. Sumiye wanted to climb to her mother's breast, but I took her away. The poor baby cried and cried. I didn't know what to do. I didn't know if I was awake or dreaming. Maybe this was all a dream. I will wake, and my mother will wake, and we will laugh at the horrible dream. 'Please, Buddha, let this be only a dream,' I asked, but I knew in my heart that my mother was dead, and it was my fault. Yes, I should have gone for the doctor. My karma is so bad. I was a bad person in a former life, so I suffer now."

My mother had witnessed many funerals but had never prepared a body for the holy rites. Now she had to, and her grief so overwhelmed her that she forcibly held her trembling hands against her body as she approached her mother's body on the slab of wood set up in the rear of the temple. The village women and some classmates arrived, and they washed the body with water blessed by my grandfather. They began with the face, and my mother was allowed to wet her mother's lips, the initial sacred rite. She was grateful that her mother appeared tranquil. They dressed her in a white kimono and placed her in a plain wooden box. My mother placed the sleeves of one of my grandmother's kimonos under her mother's head as a support and the remaining panels as a covering for her lower body. No one objected to the splashes of color.

"I felt like fainting… I felt like crying… but I kept working," my mother said. "No tears, none. I wanted to be strong for Honorable Father. I wanted him to be proud of me."

She heard the women whispering, "*Kawaisou ni, kawaisou ni!* What a pity, what a pity! So young. Poor Yoshiko-chan with three young children to care for. What a pity." My mother did feel sorry for herself. Yes, what was she going to do? How would she cope? What was going to happen to all of them?

She didn't remember much about the funeral. Two monks arrived from neighboring villages and added to the confusion with extra sutra chanting that seemed to go on and on. The herbalist lady had to remind her twice when it was time to offer incense. My mother walked to the altar with

My grandmother, Sen Hayashi Iwatake (seated), holding my mother, with her sister, Kisayo Ogawa, about 1903. This was a precious picture for my mother. It is the only existing photograph of her mother and her aunt.

clay feet and stared at the smoke spiraling from the thin green sticks. She didn't know what to do or why she was standing in front of the image of the Golden Buddha with her mother in a box and all these people behind her in black and quietly weeping. The herbalist woman whispered something, put the rosary around her hands, told her to bow, and led her back to her seat.

My mother refused to accompany the body to the cremation chamber, a large brick oven tucked into another part of the village. She couldn't bear to watch her mother engulfed in flames. Her mother's ashes were buried behind the temple beneath a simple marker.

When she cried at the funeral, her father told her, "Shed all your tears now because after today there will be no time for crying. You will set a good example for the village people." So my mother vowed to be a model mother and guardian to her three younger siblings. She would never give anyone reason to criticize or gossip about her family. And she would never allow people to witness her crying. And so my mother's childhood ended. She was twelve.

For one week, her father conducted a daily memorial service, then another one on the forty-ninth day after the funeral. Her mother's soul was now securely in nirvana, Buddha willing, or, alternately, in another earthly body if it were not deemed pure enough to rest forever with the Ultimate. My mother was certain her mother's soul was peacefully in heaven.

For a few weeks, neighboring women helped my mother settle into daily chores, but they, too, had family responsibilities, and soon—too quickly—she became the full-fledged keeper of the house. She sacrificed her own schooling—managing to attend only intermittently—and tried to make sure her younger brothers met and followed the standards of a priest's family.

My mother's daily life was probably not much different from that of early-twentieth-century Japanese rural families, but because of the singular status of her father as Buddhist leader, the expectations were higher. Her life was filled with shoulds, musts, and ought to's, words that filtered into my life like prayers.

•

The hospital at Amache was still under construction. My mother and I stepped around wires and loose boards tossed carelessly on the floor and found my grandmother, pale but awake. She stared at me for a long time. Finally, my mother had to explain who I was: "This is Yuriko."

"Misa, you came," she whispered. My grandmother mistook me for her daughter, Misako Frances.

"Obah-san," I interrupted, "I hope you'll be well soon. Then maybe the government will let you go live with Misako in Salt Lake."

Neither my mother nor I knew any more words of consolation. My aunt and her husband, Ken, had been two of the fortunate people able to move inland before the mass evacuation began. Ken worked for the Fujiya Farm Equipment Company, which allowed its employees to take advantage of the ten-day grace period mandated by the government to scout for a location willing to "receive the enemy." Most cities and towns, especially smaller ones, refused refuge. But Salt Lake City already had some small Japanese enclaves, mostly Mormon, and Ab Jenkins, the mayor, gave his consent. The Fujiya Farm Equipment Company formed an automobile convoy of ten vehicles (traveling in a lone car would be dangerous) and arrived in the city in February of 1942. As far as I knew, Misako and Ken had little contact with Grandfather and Grandmother Nakai.

My grandmother was tiny and appeared fragile, but her mouth was tight and determined. She was, after all, a survivor. She seldom smiled. When I was four or five, my grandparents had lived close to the White King soap factory. When I even thought about their small apartment, I associated it with the gagging stink—a dead animal smell—that wafted from that processing plant. I dreaded those infrequent, but obligatory, visits to my grandparents because I was sure I would throw up from the insidious odor. Obah-san always offered tea and rice crackers, but the sight of them made my stomach churn. My mother had reprimanded me for refusing the treat— such bad manners—so on subsequent trips, I took some, politely thanked my grandmother, and pretended to nibble on one.

Some years later, they moved into a house next door to us with my aunts, Misako Frances and Mitsuko Evelyn. They were both in high school, so I rarely saw them, except for the few times they babysat me. Once they thought my hair was "too Japanese" and proceeded to give me curls. They wet strips of cloth and wrapped my hair around them until everything dried. When they finally undid the bundles, I had springy, wienerlike curls. My mother laughed and laughed—but in a nice way—and thanked my aunts for turning me into Shirley Temple's twin. *"Kawaii,"* she said. "Cute." My grandmother said nothing. The next morning my hair was straight again.

Many years later, I thought about my father's mother and her cold attitude. She had married at sixteen and had never attended school in Japan because girls were thought to be fit only for childbearing, raising children, and laboring on the farm. Perhaps Grandmother Nakai didn't know how to express nurturing because she had never received any. She neglected my father because that was what she had experienced as a child; it was the only parenting model she had had in her life. I felt sorry for her, but I was also alienated from her. Neither of us made an effort to bond closer to each other.

I suspected that she had not provided much more loving care to her two daughters born in the United States. "We didn't talk much to each other," Aunt Frances told me. "My father and mother never learned English, and we never learned Japanese. They were so busy just trying to survive that they didn't have time for anything beyond that."

When my aunts graduated from high school and moved away to live with other families while attending trade school, my grandparents moved to San Juan Capistrano to try farming again. My grandfather's first job in America was as a day laborer on a farm run by another Issei. He lived in a dormitory and cooked communally over an outside fire. He soon found that he boiled rice better than he plowed and volunteered to become *dorei kukku,* "cook of slaves." The farmers felt like slaves. They worked from dawn to dusk with only short breaks for meals, which my grandfather ladled out hurriedly, knowing they would be reprimanded for dawdling. Later, my grandparents rented a small portion of the farm and eked out a living.

Our trips to the farm were an adventure, at least on the road. My brother and I were allowed to ride in the rumble seat of our old Ford. My mother prepared a lunch of rice balls, chicken, and a big jug of lemonade for the two-hour journey. At the outskirts of Los Angeles, orange and lemon groves framed both sides of the road...miles and miles of trees dotted with yellow and orange fruit. Then appeared patches and rows of low green plants—potatoes, tomatoes and peppers with grape vines tenderly twining around rungs of wire. Each mile startled me with new colors—olive, cobalt, emerald, a brilliant yellow, chalk white—and endless contours and profiles—bumpy, curved, sharp, stooped. I loved to pretend I was watching a movie—a Technicolor one, presented just for me, an audience of one. My family didn't understand when I tried to explain what I saw. *"Nani?* What? You're nuts," my brother always retorted.

We unwrapped the rice balls and tossed out the waxed paper, which danced into the road or gully; we were heedless of litter in that era of wide-open spaces. One time the paper whipped into the windshield of the car following us, and the driver swerved. I ducked, hoping he hadn't noticed me. The car sped up, and, as it passed, the driver honked—*ga-goo-ga*—and angrily shook his fist. When we arrived at the farm, my father asked why the man had appeared so angry. I meekly explained that a piece of waxed paper had hit his windshield.

I expected a scolding, but my father only said, "Well, next time be more careful." With a sigh of relief, I bounded into the house, shouting, "Obah-san, we're here. We're here. We've come to see you." That was the day when I was shooed outside and hurt my knee.

At Amache my grandmother was soon released from the hospital. However, she was even more taciturn when my mother and I visited her. She said nothing beyond "hello." My grandfather, too, appeared worn and tired. He mumbled about the weather and his wife's condition, then fell silent. My mother encouraged my grandmother: *"Ganbatte, ne;* hold on," but fearing more depressing silence, we left, promising to visit again soon. My mother may have gone, but I never did.

4

Stepping toward Freedom

SPAGHETTI ON A HOT PLATE

And so we braved the winter, and one day it was spring of 1943, barely a year since our forced evacuation. There was no leisurely transition of seasons in this wild place. One day it was cold and blustery, the next day warm and sunny. We opened our windows, washed the scum from the panes, and tossed the ossified clumps of cloth we had stuffed in the cracks. "Should we wash and save them for next year?" my mother wondered. We shoveled ashes from the potbellied stove but allowed the tea kettle to squat primly on the top, not to labor as a humidifier as it had done all winter. My mother even polished the protruding belly until it shone.

"Why bother with that?" I asked her.

"*Shunki oosouji*—spring cleaning. In Japan we do this before the New Year. Clean everything. Wash everything. So everything is fresh and bright."

I looked around. Fresher maybe, but bright it was not. Perhaps cheerier than when we had first moved in because my mother and I had added cotton curtains and painted the partitions a glowing white. The walls were still turd tan, stained now with watermarks undulating beneath the windows and the rifts between the wall and ceiling. The floor sported some small mottled rugs that my mother had braided from strips torn from donated and discarded blankets. They provided some relief from the shock of the frigid brick floor on icy mornings.

On the walls, I had tacked pictures from magazines: Elizabeth Taylor at the foot of my bed, some landscapes with palm trees by the door, and,

PROMISE, WATERCOLOR, 22 BY 30 INCHES.
In a dream, a ghostly girl steps from a picture frame and floats away. Faint figures in various states
of torment draw themselves into the background debris. The barbed wire morphs into Japanese calligraphy
at the bottom of the painting.

best of all, a roiling ocean over the shelf with our toothbrushes. We found no way to disguise the bare bulb in the middle of the room, and so it hung there, testament to the architectural nakedness of these barracks.

A month before our great oosouji, my mother had noted my birthday. I turned eleven. "Happy Birthday, Yuri," she said. "Next year we'll have a nice party." After dinner my mother produced a box of Ritz crackers and proceeded to spread strawberry jam on one, peanut butter on another, and stacked four or five. She offered the mound to me. "This is like a little cake," she said. "Happy birthday." I wondered if she knew how much I loved her at that moment. Looking back now, I wish I had told her.

My brother and I shared the same birthday date two years apart, so we always celebrated with a single cake in Los Angeles. The Harringtons honored us with the birthday cake, a huge one with thick white waves of frosting. Moreover, it was ringed with fantastic sugar animals—a giraffe, a tiger, an elephant, a parrot, a zebra, and a monkey, each one painstakingly detailed in realistic color.

When we picked up the cake, Mrs. Harrington explained the animals' significance: "The giraffe is tall and strong, and my wish is for Prince to grow up tall and strong. Yoshiko was born in the Year of the Tiger, so that one's for her. The parrot is our Polly. Your father can't ever make up his mind, so he's the black-and-white zebra. The monkey is you, Yuriko, because you're always running around, and besides, Yoshiko says you were born in the Year of the Monkey. And the elephant never forgets. I'll always remember all of you; you're my family."

I coveted the giraffe, the biggest of all the animals. On that birthday before the war, I teasingly reached for it and pinched the neck. Sumiya's hand shot out. He grabbed the body, and the giraffe snapped in two.

"Look what you've done!" my brother cried and threw his piece on the table. "You can have the dumb thing." He ran from the room.

I was horrified. How I wished I could rewind those few seconds. I had ruined everything. I sat motionless in my chair and held back tears. My mother and I tried to attach the pieces by wetting the edges and pushing the body together. I left it by my brother's place at the table, but he ignored it. It sat there the next day and the next until my mother "disappeared" it.

At Amache no one—at least not anyone inside the camp, nor anyone my age—had a birthday party or cake. Nevertheless, I wondered, fleetingly, if Mrs. Harrington would magically manage to send us a cake, but, of course, nothing arrived.

I attended a different sort of birthday celebration during the final year at Amache. Elizabeth, a fair-haired student, was part of our seventh-grade class. She lived on the other side of the barbed-wire boundary in a white clapboard house, part of a complex for "those others," the Caucasian employees. None of us befriended her…her presence puzzled us. Most of the white children attended schools in Granada or Lamar. Was she a child spy, tattling on us to the authorities? We were always suspicious and spoke to her guardedly.

Elizabeth invited all the girls to her birthday party. By 1945 the authorities had decided it was safe to do so—we would not run away. Probably the gesture was deemed a humanitarian act so we might once more become accustomed to the outside and its civilities.

The party was strained. We shared cake and ice cream and played some games. Then Elizabeth announced she had a wonderful surprise. We followed her outside and came face-to-face with…a horse! A horse!

"You can all have turns riding Ranger," she said, her eyes beaming.

We can? I don't think so. I had never been so close to an honest-to-goodness horse. This creature was huge. My face was even with its rump. I had no intention of riding it. When my turn came, I hesitated.

"Thank you, but I'll skip my turn," I said.

"Oh, we all have to have this experience," Elizabeth's mother exclaimed. "Ranger is very gentle. Here give him this carrot and show him you're his friend."

I reluctantly took the carrot and stretched out my hand. The horse slobbered all over it. I stooped and wiped the muck on the grass.

"I don't want to…," I began, but Elizabeth held the stirrup and urged me to place my foot into it. "Left foot. Then swing the right over."

How did you gracefully arc your leg over the backside of a gigantic beast? If we had been warned beforehand, I would have worn trousers.

My right leg barely slid over to the other side. Unbalanced, I grabbed the horse's mane and tugged. Ranger sensed my bumbling, and—just as I seated myself—he reared and triumphantly neighed. I clung to him for dear life. I was sure Ranger was going to gallop off "into the sunset," but there was no Lone Ranger to come to the rescue. I screamed.

Elizabeth helped me off. "What did you do? He's never done that before," she said accusingly. I sat alone for the remainder of the party. I have never ridden a horse since.

·

I remembered that we always celebrated my mother's birthday on September 8. She requested that this date be etched on her grave marker. "But," she said, "my real birthday is September 1."

"Why don't we celebrate it then?" I asked.

"Because my birth certificate says September 8." Every year on September 1, my mother reminded me: "Today is my real birthday, but we'll wait a week to celebrate it." I didn't get it.

Finally, one day my mother told me a story. She had been born at home in a rectory attached to my grandfather's Buddhist Church in Mirasaka, a hamlet of farms inland from Hiroshima. It was a long trek to the registry office, she recalled, maybe ten or fifteen miles. As with most village priests at the turn of the twentieth century, my grandfather Iwatake eked out a meager living from small donations and presiding at funerals and weddings. He owned two pairs of footwear: a Sunday pair of *tabi* stockings with thick soles and a second pair of straw sandals for daily wear. My grandmother had patched and repaired the straw sandals with yarn or straw until they resembled nothing more than wasted straps. If the villagers noticed, they said nothing. It meant a sacrifice on their part to offer more than the few sen they tossed into the donation bowl. They had nothing more to give. Mostly they bartered services.

"My father was ashamed to visit the village in ragged footwear," my mother explained with a catch in her throat, "and too proud to ask the sandal maker for credit. The morning after I was born, my father found a pair of Western shoes on the *genkan*. Think of that. Shoes! Nobody wore shoes then, only rich city people. Father asked the midwife, but she didn't know anything. Maybe the villagers had bought them. Maybe somebody had stolen them. My father thought that perhaps Buddha had answered his prayer.

"But the shoes were too tight; Japanese feet are very wide. So for a week, my father stretched the shoes by moistening them and then walking in them. They were still much too tight when he walked off to register my birth. He left at dawn and returned after dark. He came home unable to walk for two days. Poor father. My mother massaged his feet all day."

My grandmother blamed this incident for my grandfather's lifelong limp. She had begged him not to go, but he had insisted—Yoshiko was his firstborn child. She told my mother, "He walked all the way to the next village for you. For you—a mere baby girl. Maybe for a boy, it is different. *Bikko o hiite,* he walked. Limping, he went." My grandmother blamed my mother for her father's lameness.

I refused to believe that this single incident could maim my grandfather's feet and cause a permanent limp, but my grandmother claimed it was true. It was even more vexing for my grandmother because the exact date of my mother's birth was of little consequence. At that time, all babies were considered to be a year old at birth and then had a birthday with everyone else in Japan on New Year's Day. So although my mother was actually only four months old, she was considered to be two years old on New Year's Day the following year.

So in choosing September 8, not September 1, my mother celebrated her father's tenacity and, I'm sure, proof of his love for her. Perhaps she also saw the gesture as atonement for her guilt for causing her father to suffer a lame foot. She could now imagine her father in heaven shod in new sandals, striding proud and tall and straight, walking without a limp.

•

One day in early spring, my father reappeared in Amache. When I returned from school, there he was, stooping over his gaping suitcase.

"Daddy!" I yelled, "You're back!"

He turned. "Hello, Yuri-chan. You've grown."

Why do you sound so distant? I've grown? Yes, I've grown. It's been a half year since you last saw me. You only wrote once, telling us you had arrived at Seabrook Farms. Then nothing. Mom wrote you letters, but they were returned with "Addressee Unknown" on them. We worried. Where were you? Why didn't you write? Don't you care about us?

I was about to voice my complaints when I noticed a square package by his suitcase. My father squatted and carefully untied it, revealing a gleaming hot plate. "Here, I brought you and Mama something," he said.

He waited for a reply. I was speechless.

So I was wrong. You did think about us. I'm ashamed to have had those bad thoughts about you, but what was I to think? It still would have been nice to have had news about you.

"We cook our own meals at Seabrook, so I bought two of these and left one for the men. I'll show you how to make quick spaghetti," he continued.

"We're not supposed to cook in the barracks, Daddy. What if they catch us?"

"Sometimes cheating is OK."

"What?"

"When people treat you like *kuso,* it's all right to break the law."

"What!"

What sort of moral lesson was this? Break the law! But sometimes I felt the same way…defy the big shots when they tried to erase us. But actually to break a law…? I wanted to ask my father if he had been one of the protesters at Santa Anita who had not been arrested and sent away, but he was already walking toward the mess hall. I followed. When we emerged, we toted a bag of food.

He draped an extension cord to the ceiling light socket and plugged in the hot plate. The coils flushed crimson. My father brought water to a boil in a small bucket and plopped in the spaghetti—"make a circle with thumb to third finger…that's the amount you want." He dug out a knife from his toolbox, honed it on a gritty block until it shone, then pressed his thumb against the blade and announced that it was fine for the job at hand. He chopped onion, green pepper, two stalks of celery, and a clove of garlic. He reached into the bag and produced a small fistful of chopped meat. I had heard rumors that we were fed horse meat, and even dog meat, but I didn't ask about the variety of this chunk he held. What had he bargained for this prize? I didn't ask that, either. We drained the spaghetti and used the same bucket for our sauce. "Use this much lard"…he scooped a fingerful…"and when it's hot, dump everything else in, cook eight minutes, add this can of tomato sauce, and you have a fine dinner."

I'm sure all our neighbors were salivating from the aroma wafting from our room, but no one interrupted our meal. My mother returned home as my father was stirring the sauce, but she did not register any surprise. "Ah, you are home," she said. My father divided the mixture into three metal bowls. I ran my fingers around the pot to get every speck. We slurped noisily.

My brother came home as I was carrying the pot and dishes to wash in the laundry room. "What'd I miss?" he asked.

"Dad's home and made some spaghetti."

"Yeah, he likes to cook. He even ran a restaurant before we were born."

"I didn't know that."

"You don't know a lot of things."

"So?"

"You don't know that Dad has a pilot's license, for one thing."

"Come again?"

"Airplane. Fly. Pilot's license. What don't you understand?"

"How'd he manage that?"

"Well, it was before he got married, so he probably saved some money."

"I want to fly a plane someday."

"Wish on," my brother said and walked into the barrack.

As I rinsed the utensils, I recalled those meals my father had made before the war. When my mother had an occasional late appointment with a dressmaking client, he took over and served sukiyaki, spaghetti, or maybe eggs and

My father. He posed reluctantly for my mother, telling her, "It's no use."

bacon. Once he fried trout whole—innards and all. My father ate the complete fish. I carefully scooped out the guts and cut off the head and fins.

"At least eat the *o-meme,* the eyes," he said. "They'll make your eyes strong. You should eat the whole head. It will make you smart."

So I plucked out the white eyeballs and chewed on them. The center kernels crunched like tiny pebbles. I spit them out.

My father watched out of the corner of his eye.

I held the head and nibbled at the jagged gill edge. It had the consistency of brittle cardboard. I sucked on it for a minute, extracting the taste of the soy sauce, but I couldn't continue when the gills crackled as I bit into them. I placed the head next to the convoluted intestines. My father reached over—a tiny grin on his face—and ate the head in a few noisy bites.

"Here you can have the rest, too," I said and pushed my plate toward him.

"Save for later. Don't waste food," he told me. Did he mean for me or for him?

"No way, José," I said.

My father carefully wrapped the leftover in waxed paper and placed it on top of the block of ice in our icebox.

That memorable spaghetti dinner in camp was the first and last meal made on that precious hot plate. A few days later, it disappeared.

The Fence

Amache High School was completed in April 1943. I had watched its progress all winter after school, walking up the slope through an empty lot to the work site. That open space in the middle of the camp was a mystery, but children found it an ideal play space for baseball, tag, red rover, marbles, kites or simply sitting on the ground and chatting. It was ideal, that is, when the weather was warm and dry. After rain and snow, it quickly turned into a quagmire of lethal mud that threatened to suck off my shoes.

At the building site, workmen mixed cement in wheelbarrows for the foundation. They mixed, and they poured, mixed and poured…for days. Their shoes and pants were crusted with chunks of cement. Their faces became pocked as if they had a mysterious disease. But they were cheerful and shouted and hollered as they shoveled and tamped the cement: "Oi, more over here," "A monster you're looking like," "Same, you!" "Quit jabbering and stir, guys."

One day two-by-fours jutted up from the foundation. Wooden crosses braced the beams, some leaning tiredly sideways. The men sawed and hammered, most of them with cigarettes dangling from their lips. They'd carelessly drop the stub, and, with a studied twist, crush it into a blurry swirl on the ground. One man chewed tobacco, the brown juice dribbling from the corner of his mouth. I looked quickly away; the sight made my stomach churn. I was thankful he spat the unsavory mess out of sight onto the dirt.

When snow fell, work stopped, but a few days later—when the wood steamed in the sharp sun—the men resumed their labor. When I next returned, the roof was almost framed—slats of wood pitched gently down in rows from end to end. They cast prison-bar shadows on the men working below. Their clothes mimicked jail uniforms.

After Christmas, rooms took shape, and I dared to walk around. Some workmen glanced curiously, but no one stopped me. There—at one end of the building—was the auditorium-to-be. The orchestra had been promised practice time in this space. A classmate named Tak and I were part of the high-school orchestra, she on the sax, and I on the piano. We were the only elementary-school students in the orchestra, and the other members usually ignored us, but once in a while some boys whispered rude comments behind us:

"Hey, baby, let's have some afterward." "Yeah, suck on that reed, kid. Wet it good." "Pound on those ivories, baby; baby, oh, oh, baby."

Their words made our cheeks burn. I was sure they held sexual connotations, but neither Tak nor I knew exactly what they meant. I was grateful that Mr. Hinman, the music teacher, always had kind words for us.

"All right, students, tune up. Yuriko, an A." He smiled. The instruments buzzed and growled like animals: bees here, bears there. Even a hyena moaned in the back. I struck A again and again until we sounded one great octave, as if communing on some huge instrument yet to be invented. Now we were ready. Mr. Hinman smiled again. "Thank you. We're so lucky to have a wonderful pianist and a super sax player. Now, let's review."

Until the new school was completed, we held rehearsals in Terry Hall, competing with the wind whistling through the window sashes. Dust ground into the valves and keys. Once I wet some dirty keys and wiped them with the edge of my sleeve. The dust congealed into paste and stuck between the keys. I had to dig it clean with a borrowed penknife.

Back at the construction site, I watched a man as he uncoiled reels of copper wire bound with braided fabric. The spirals writhed like serpents until the electrician tamed them. He pulled and led them through the slats and imprisoned them with nails. Power raced through these for lights, hot plates, shavers, refrigerators, and washing machines...that is, if we had had them here. What a staggering insight. I looked up and followed strands of thick wire lacing into T-poles. The wires draped toward other poles and, farther on, more poles until they stitched into the horizon.

I hurried home. "Daddy, where does that electricity come from? There are all these wires strung on poles that just go on and on. When we were on the train, the poles and wires followed us almost all the way. I didn't think about it until now. How does that happen, all that power?"

My father looked at me curiously. "Why do you need to know? Girls don't need to learn such things. *Tsumaranai,* useless stuff."

"Wires, then electricity. It's magic."

"There must be a power plant somewhere. They use coal that makes heat that makes energy. Then they push that through the wires and send it to us."

"Just like that?"

"Yes. Just like that."

Many years later, a high-school physics teacher lectured about AC/DC, atoms, generators, and transformers. I flunked that week's pop quiz. Perhaps my father was right—tsumaranai; it was useless information. I flipped a switch; the light came on. I flipped it back; the light went off. What more did I need to know?

A dedicatory assembly was held when the high school was completed. I had hoped that the orchestra would play, but instead, Mr. Hinman chose the band. Maybe the band was louder and more rousing; it had a snare drum and big brass. The Boy Scout troop marched in smartly, raised the flag, and led us in the Pledge of Allegiance. For a second, I thought some boys would make a commotion and walk out. Rather, people were beaming proudly. Perhaps the school symbolized a new beginning, a chance for that "three-times-better-than-whites" education. The auditorium was cleaner and lighter than Terry Hall, if not dust proof. We all played better despite the hollow overtones that echoed from the ceiling beams.

•

A new high school was completed in the spring of 1943. I thought it was gorgeous and was disappointed that the lower grades continued classes in converted barracks.

The dedication ceremony of the new high school. (Photo gift of Jack Muro, Japanese American National Museum 2012.2.343; reprinted by permission of the Japanese American National Museum. Copyright 2013. All rights reserved.)

Now that he was back in camp, my father reverted to his old routine and spent most of his time in the rec room playing poker or mahjong. Some of the men—equally restless—perused the papers and notices for outside jobs, and about a month later, my father announced his departure again. I was standing by the barbed-wire fence.

My father walked up and asked, "What are you staring at…by the fence again?"

I couldn't remember him ever being curious about my activities. I was even more surprised that he had noticed my visits to the periphery of camp. "I…I'm…," I stammered, "I'm just wondering what's out there."

Actually I was vaguely remembering Mexico. When I was very small—perhaps two or three—my father had taken me and Sumiya there, probably to Tijuana. I only recalled some towering fountains that spilled water from their tops. I had sat on the tiled edge of the pool surrounding one and splashed the frothy water with my feet, then dipped my arms and scooped the water backward, showering my father. He had laughed and jumped into the pool with my brother, and we had leaped and stamped until we were sopping wet. How we laughed and laughed! I wanted more than anything to laugh again with my father.

"Yuri, you think I don't care about you and Sumiya. And…and Mama," he added. *He was seriously talking to me. To me! What was prompting this?*

"So, do you? Do you care?"

"I'm going to try another outside job. See, I can make at least fourteen dollars a week, and if they'll take me as a carpenter, thirty-eight. I'll send money to Mama, and you can buy some nice things and save up for when you get out."

"You didn't answer my question. Do you care?"

"Why do you think I'm going to try to find an outside job?"

"Why?"

"I told you. I want you all to have money so you can buy things you need, things you want."

"Daddy, it's crappy here, really crappy, but we don't need swell stuff. We can think about that when we get out. Stay with us."

"I can't. Look at this place. I didn't come to America to live in a place like this—stuffed like pigs in pens. What does the government think we are? Animals?"

"Stay with us," I appealed again.

"Look where we are. In nowhere America." My father's voice bristled with resentment. "We get treated like dirt. You and Sumiya are American

My brother and me in Mexico, probably in Tijuana, in 1934.

citizens, for God's sake, and you get pushed around, put into a prison camp. What the hell kind of life is this? Soldiers with rifles, stupid searchlights...?"

"Daddy, can't you...?"

"Stop! My ears hurt. I told you. I'm going out again." His tone announced finality.

"Do you remember when we went to Mexico?" I asked him then.

"No."

"When I was little."

"Maybe."

"We had so much fun, Daddy."

My father's reply surprised me. His voice got soft. "We'll have fun again, Yuri; *shinbou sena*. Be patient and wait. We'll go to Mexico again."

THROUGH THE GAPS, WATERCOLOR, 22 BY 30 INCHES.
Our single room was lit by one bare bulb. Moths were attracted to it, and each morning I found scores of them
scattered across the brick floor.

When he walked away, I wondered if he honestly meant what he said. Would we go to Mexico? Could I be patient? Could I wait? I had no choice.

I peered into the desert, willing it to sparkle, but it lay unyielding with endless puffs of sage and clumps of prickly cacti. The panorama was monotonous but strangely hypnotic. Sometimes if I gazed long enough, the grays and greens slivered into shimmering layers and trembled like lake water. But the magic didn't happen now.

Suddenly, I felt eyes watching me. I glanced up at the guard tower about fifty feet away. The soldier waved. A prickle ran down my arms. Was he waving a warning? Was I too close to the fence? I stepped back but just as quickly moved forward again toward the stupid barrier. I felt a surge of fear but also one of defiance. The imprisonment was unfair. The fence, the barracks, the tower—everything was unfair.

With a soft crunch of footsteps, someone whispered, "Hey, there."

I jumped in fright and instinctively grabbed the wire of the fence. A barb pierced my palm with a hot shock. I was too frightened to let go and watched the blood drip off my hand onto the sand.

"Don't be scared. Here let me see your hand," the voice said.

I turned. It was the guard, rifle still cradled on his shoulder. He stood close enough that I could see the stubble on his chin. He was grinning.

"You're bleeding. You shouldn't have done that with your pretty little hand. Take this," he offered. It was his handkerchief—khaki like everything else on him.

Still, I couldn't move. My hand was glued to the wire.

The guard reached for my frozen hand.

Just then, in the distance, I heard my father yelling, "Get away from her, you sonofabitch." He whipped past the barracks faster than I had ever seen anyone run. His voice shattered the air: "Get away!" The guard whirled, whipped the rifle off his shoulder, and gripped it at his side. My father kept running and yelling, "Get away! Get away, you sonofabitch" as he approached us.

I released my hands and reached for my father. He grabbed them, and I held on. I gripped his hands and wouldn't let go because I knew that if I did, he would lunge at the soldier.

"You've got it all wrong," the soldier said. Then he shrugged his shoulders and sauntered back to the guard tower. We watched him climb the ladder. When he reached the cubicle, he waved.

"Kuso baka," my father swore at the guard. Then he warned me, "Don't go that near the fence again, Yuri. See what happens?"

That evening the block chairman announced a meeting in the mess hall. A few people wanted my parents to report the incident to the camp police. Both my mother and father claimed they didn't want trouble, that I had learned my lesson. That first year in Amache, I had heard of some skirmishes between guards and evacuees. At one time, rumors flew that two murdered bodies had been found in a barrack, but nothing came of the news. The police claimed it was a bogus story. It was safer, easier, to keep the water unruffled. *Shikataganai.*

"When a white man says something, and a Japanese says another, you know who the government will believe," my father said. Most of the people agreed. The meeting broke up with grumbling, and some men swore at my father, telling him he was a banana—yellow skin but all white inside.

My father left camp a few days after the meeting. "Mind your mother," he said as he climbed onto the truck.

I thought about the soldier episode. Although I had been frightened, I remembered a shiver of excitement. What if I had accepted the handkerchief? Would the soldier have tenderly stroked my hand, then my arm? Then maybe kissed me? That's what happened in movies. The violins swelled, and the screen gradually blackened. Obviously something stirring occurred in that darkness.

No, a white man wouldn't kiss a yellow Jap, the enemy. That soldier even had a rifle, ready to shoot. I was the enemy, or why else was I here? Sumi had brought an article from a San Francisco newspaper to school that claimed we were "the dirtiest, the most despicable torturer the world has ever known" and "the scum of a warped civilization."

Mrs. Bender assured us that this was not true, but we all saw it there in a newspaper, and if it wasn't true, why would it be in print? "Just because words are written down in newspapers and books, it doesn't mean that those words are necessarily true," she explained, and she asked us to define "despicable."

SUNFLOWERS, WATERCOLOR, 30 BY 22 INCHES.
Several persevering individuals managed to create sunflower gardens despite the scarcity
of water. The orange-and-white tower held our water supply.

We knew that it was bad but not the precise meaning. She asked Sumi to check the dictionary: "deserving of contempt or scorn," she read.

"What does that mean?" Mrs. Bender asked. We didn't know exactly. When people scorned us, they didn't talk to us because they didn't like us, and when people held us in contempt, they didn't like us and looked down on us. It all amounted to the same thing. Mrs. Bender added the word to our weekly spelling list, but she also gave us "worthy" and "laudable." And made us promise to say at least ten times during the day, "I am worthy. I am laudable."

Gaman or not, summer at Amache was a season of brutal endurance. Without the softening coastal mist of L.A., the sun blazed down and bleached the sage and buildings into an even paler hue. Heat waves shimmered over the roofs and deceived my eyes into believing I saw treeless oases floating primly in the sky. *Gaman* was all we could do. Babies tottered about naked. Adults sought relief in the shade of the barracks.

I moved like a zombie when the temperatures soared above a hundred degrees. The shower was a popular place to be. So much so that a sign was posted at the entrance: "Please limit shower time to two minutes." Water was laboriously pumped into the checkered orange-and-white water tank, perched on slender stilts at the north end of camp. Sometimes only a copper-colored gurgle coughed from the spigots. Sometimes there was nothing at all.

In the desert, we discovered ants, grasshoppers, spiders, moths, centipedes, and beetles we had never known existed. Each morning I swept up the moths that had been lured indoors by our light bulb. If I jumped onto a clump of brush, a bouquet of grasshoppers wheeled into the air. Spiders, undeterred by diligent dusting, spun webs with vigor and ease in every nook and cranny. Centipedes squeezed their way between the bricks in the floors, alert for a bare foot.

When I was a youngster, I was so allergic to mosquito bites that each one puffed up into a urine-colored pustule. If I pushed on the membrane, it jiggled like Jell-O. My mother then pierced it with a needle and blotted the ooze with cotton balls. The bite itched, and—despite countless admonitions of "don't scratch"—I did. The wound sometimes became infected and suppurated down my leg. Once in Los Angeles, my shins and calves were so pocked with bites and scars that my mother allowed me to skip school and then sent me in slacks with a note explaining my absence.

"Mosquito bites?" My teacher sounded incredulous.

I pulled up my pant leg.

"Oh!" she gasped and sent me quickly to the school nurse.

The nurse sent me home.

"Why are you home?" my mother asked.

"The nurse said I'd give this to other kids."

"Mosquito bites aren't contagious. Doesn't she know better?" my mother asked with irritation.

"She said it must be something else, that bites don't look like this."

Those ugly blots gave me a week's respite from school. I followed my mother to her dressmaking clients and helped her weed and hoe our small garden and cook meals. She showed me how to darn socks and rip out a seam. We squeezed oranges to have ready for my brother when he returned from school, and one day we baked sugar cookies. I puffed with pride when Sumiya said they were delicious. He ate a half dozen.

When I returned to school—to my chagrin—I was placed in an isolation corner until my scars healed. I had to visit the nurse each day before school. I was never told what fearsome disease I was supposed to have had.

So—hoping to ward off pocked legs in camp—my mother ordered netting, green and camphor infused, from Monkey Ward, which we fashioned into mosquito nets. They were cumbersome and smelly but effective. At night I could hear the frantic whines of tiny beasts whizzing around the net, trying to find a tear, some flaw through which they might feast on my blood. Occasionally I woke with a red itchy welt, but the bites never swelled with the ferocity of those from California mosquitoes. My mother credited the desert air, which made my skin browner and thicker. I told her the Colorado varieties were puny because they bred in a place with so little water. I later learned that our camp was only a few miles from the Arkansas River, and mosquitoes multiplied in the pockets of stagnant water along its shoreline.

When I complained of the Amache heat, my mother said, "We can endure this. *Gaman.* My life in Japan at your age was hard, so much harder than this. Your life here is not so bad." She went on to recall her teenage years in Japan: "I think I go crazy," she said. She told me how each day, as she helped Tatsuzo and Junroku with homework, she placed Sumiye beside her and gave her a pencil and paper to keep her busy. My mother delighted in her sister's careful renderings of Japanese letters that Sumiye copied, untutored. Sumiye was eager to learn. Her father praised Sumiye but continually criticized Junroku's indifference. He blamed my mother. "If Sumiye can write like that at three, you can teach Junroku the same way," he said. "Make a greater effort."

My mother pressured and coaxed, but Junroku resisted. Resigned, my grandfather decided—when Junroku was eight or nine—to send him to another temple to serve the monks there and learn discipline.

"I begged father not to send him away, but he said that it was best for the family and I should not talk about it anymore. So I was quiet. I knew he would not change his mind. I told Junroku to be a good boy and study hard. We parted quietly. "No tears," my mother said, "No tears." I detected an immense sorrow in her voice.

She kept silent for years but thought constantly about her youngest brother. Finally, after Sumiye died, she made another concerted effort to bring Junroku home, but her father would not consider it—his son now belonged to the other temple, and it would be a dishonorable act to take back what had been given in good faith.

"Junroku is not merchandise to trade! He's a human being. I want him home," my mother cried. Then she added, "Please?"

"No," her father replied and walked away.

So then my mother announced her intention of moving to Hiroshima and asking the priests to release Junroku to her care. He was still only twelve, a minor. She wanted a second chance with him. She visited him, and he, too, desperately wanted to join her. Apparently his life at the temple was miserable. Although he received an excellent education, some of the priests took advantage of Junroku's naiveté and ordered him to complete menial, and sometimes superfluous, tasks—rewash the wooden floors, pick tiny twigs and leaves off the pathways, clean soiled sickroom debris—then complained to the superior about Junroku's supposed sloppiness and insubordination. As a result, he received yet more chores and a reprimand. As the youngest acolyte, he had no recourse and told my mother he cried himself to sleep many nights.

My mother stubbornly redoubled her resolve and moved to Hiroshima. She secured a steady job at a prefecture teletype office and boarded at the women's hostel. She worked from seven to three and enrolled in extension classes at a junior college. She barely had time to say good-bye and good evening to the other women. She made no friends. She wanted to become

The older of my mother's brothers, Zentatsu (née Tatsuzo) Iwatake, wearing traditional Zen Buddhist novitiate robes about 1930.

a nurse but found that without a high-school diploma, she could not be accepted into the program. She wanted to help people get well and stay healthy. "If I help one child, one mother, maybe I can save some suffering in the world," she said.

The following year Junroku was transferred to yet-another temple at Matsue, a town on the western shore of Japan. Thwarted once again, my mother angrily confronted her father. He told her the temple priest had made the decision and Junroku had been given a new temple name, Bukkai. He had had nothing to do with the new move.

However, for the remainder of her life, my mother harbored a sliver of doubt: "My father was a good man. He was a priest, so he wouldn't lie,"

My mother's younger brother, Bukkai (née Junroku) Temporin, about 1930. Adopted into his wife's family with no male heir, he took her family name.

she wondered; then she paused. "Would he? How could it be that Junroku could not leave the temple and come home? I was his real family. Oh, I don't understand why my life is so difficult, so full of sadness. It must be *bachi,* retribution. Am I such an evil person?"

My mother was always invoking karma and retribution as the answers to life's major and minor problems. The refrain could get tiresome. "Maybe it's not karma, Mom, just bad luck. Maybe reincarnation has nothing to do with it," I ventured. "What if all this stuff about rebirth isn't true?"

My mother looked at me thoughtfully and was quiet. When she spoke, she didn't contradict me. "Maybe," she said. "Maybe. If Junroku had come to Hiroshima, and I had become a nurse, I would not have married your

生　徒　朝　會　整　列

The Japanese school student body in Los Angeles before the war.

daddy. Maybe there was another path. Maybe life is only lucky and unlucky. Maybe life is a big game of chance. Maybe there is no karma. So then there is no Buddha, no Christians, no God. Maybe we just die and our spirits die with us. Is that what you think?"

Was she teasing me, making fun of me? I had no answer. I didn't know.

PHYLA ETCETERA

No matter where we were—even in a prison camp—schooling took precedence, that is, after food and a place to sleep. In Los Angeles, I had attended Saturday Japanese school. The *nihongakko* consisted of every-day-after-school students and Saturday students, and naturally the EDAS ones were ahead of us in every way—reading, writing, and calligraphy. We once-a-week students were branded second rate and assigned front-row seats "to better hear *sensei.*" Before class began, the student body lined up in perfect

A page from a Japanese school textbook.

rows in the yard behind the building and listened to the exhortations of the principal. One morning he cited the example of a diligent student who had used lunch hour to study, rather than take a break to eat. I suddenly realized he was talking about me. In reality I had been frantically pouring over the *kanji,* the Japanese characters, that were on a test after lunch and which I had forgotten to study. I was scrawling them over and over, hoping that my hand would click into automatic mode. The principal had walked in, nodded, and muttered, "Um, *kanshin,* admirable," and walked out again. I doubt he knew or even cared who I was; he had just seen a student laboring furiously and assumed I was conscientious. Wouldn't he have been surprised to learn he had been praising a slacker?!

Unlike Lockwood Street School, recess here was subdued. The school was located in a shabby ghetto neighborhood, and we were admonished to play quietly. "We want no complaints from our friends. We must show them that the Japanese are respectful," we were told. I spent the time drawing pictures—mostly faces with big eyes—and giving them away to my friends. I even audaciously signed my name as if I were a for-real artist. Or, surrounded by these same friends, I told mystery stories, made up on the spot and always to be continued the next week: a girl enters a haunted house behind a squeaking door like the one on the radio program, *Inner Sanctum,* and encounters strange visions and noises.

"Cre.... . eeee.... . ak," I whispered. "The girl slowly opens the door. Cobwebs hang down everywhere and tangle in her hair. She feels something move on her head." I dramatically jumped off my seat. "A spider! Hundreds of them." I nattered on and on, moving the protagonist through countless dark rooms until she reaches the top floor and, of course, finds more closed doors with scary beings and ghosts lurking behind them. The heroine always got away safely and usually found a companion girl to accompany her.

I didn't mind Japanese school, to the disbelief of my friends, especially Helen.

"Well," she said, "my mother told me that kids like you usually goof around at Japanese school and don't take it seriously, and so you don't learn a lot."

I wasn't sure what "kids like you" meant, so all I managed to protest was, "Oh, yeah?"

I loved my canvas *kaban,* briefcase, that always smelled Japanese, no matter how old it became. And I loved the graceful loops and curves of *hiragana,* those cursive letters, and tried hard to copy the scrolls and circular symbols with their soft hooks at the ends. We were just beginning brush calligraphy when the war broke out. I was forced to give up my *sumi* ink block and big brush.

•

Now, in a desert environment, the Amache school administration offered summer enrichment classes but, of course, not Japanese. I assume the offerings were designed to keep us occupied. I signed up for carpentry but was told it was for boys only. One boy scoffed, "Don't you know that?" I had visualized the surprise on my father's face when I told him I knew how to saw a proper cut and clamp pieces with Elmer's wood glue to make sturdy joints. We could do our "together thing."

Disappointed, I enrolled in Nature Study and Tonette, then Sewing. The tonette and sewing classes were a cinch. Tonette scores were one-note-at-a-time music. C-C-G-G-A-A-G, "Twinkle, Twinkle, Little Star," not the complicated chords of piano music. In sewing I stitched a dirndl skirt and then spent the other weeks helping students with their aprons.

The nature-study class was something else. We imprisoned bugs in a cylindrical bottle reeking with an evil smell. The teacher said that arthropods were the most abundant animals in the world and we could capture many of them right outside our barracks near the fence. Arthropod was a phylum, a division in science. So there were arachnids—spiders, gryllidae— crickets, chilopoda—centipedes, and other odd crawly things.

I pinned the bugs on a board and, below them, neatly pasted ID tags in my newfound knowledge, that mysterious Latin lingo. My prize, centered on the board, was a furry tarantula—family: Theraphosidae, order: Araneae.

"Lily, tarantulas don't live this far north. Are you sure you found it here?" The teacher sounded dubious.

Where else would I get it? Do you think I slipped away to Arizona, then carried my prize here by pony express? Or that I sprouted wings and flew to New Mexico? Are you accusing me of cheating?

"What do you know anyway," I blurted. I was immediately sorry when I saw his dumbfounded look. Of course he knew a lot, and tarantulas probably weren't native to Colorado.

At the end of the month, I lined up my display with the others for an Open House. However, my father was "outside," my mother was teaching a class that afternoon, and my brother—probably busy with his friends— didn't come. Before I returned to my barrack, I detoured to the far end of our block and, without aim, whirled the board over the barbed-wire fence as far as I could throw it.

•

Of course, after school we indulged in games. The summer heat was a challenge, so outdoor games began at dusk. "Annie, Annie, over," we chanted as we tossed a tired tennis ball over a barrack. Eva, Tami, Katy, and I usually stood on one side with other friends—and we even let boys play—on the other side. The aim was to catch the ball, dash with it to the other side, and tag someone. The muted light created a sinister mood as if we were chanting a spell, attempting to raise dead spirits from a hulking mausoleum.

I tossed the ball. It swished, then tapped down the other side of the roof: *koton, koton . . . ton . . . . . ton . . . . t;* "t . . . to . . rise . . up, up from your grave . . ."; *koton, koton . . . ton . . . t.*

Then silence. Did they catch the ball? Did they miss? Are they sneaking around the side? Where? This side? Then in a burst, the catchers swamped us. Who has the ball? It was too late to wonder as one of us was tagged.

We played over and over.

Koton, koton . . . ton . . . . . ton . . . . . t . . . . t.

Only when the ball blended with the evening dark did we quit.

We also had other games. I had my jacks and found that the cement floor of the laundry room was the ideal surface to play. It was relatively smooth but more importantly, it was cool. "We're too old for this," we said, but we kept playing. The jacks twinkled into constellations on the gray floor. And although we wiped the floor before playing, we swiped sand with every swoop. We played until our hands were sooty or a woman claimed the space for her laundry.

Baseball games convened in the field south of the high school, and if we chose the right moment, the boys might allow us to take a position, usually in the outfield. However, the field was often populated by boys and girls from other blocks, so we were relegated to the status of fretful spectators and soon returned to our block. A volleyball game might be in progress. A net was strung between the barracks, and no one complained of the dust and noise we raised. Sometimes adults joined us, and we were surprised by their agility. They were so old—in their twenties and thirties.

AND WE DANCED WITH FRED AND GINGER, WATERCOLOR, 22 BY 30 INCHES.
Each Saturday night, and sometimes on Thursdays, we saw movies in the mess hall. In this painting,
I transformed Fred Astaire and Ginger Rogers into Japanese dancers.

I claimed the comics page from the papers in the rec hall as soon as people were finished reading it. My funny-paper heroine was Brenda Starr, glamorous reporter. When she appeared in a particularly fetching evening dress, spangled and full, I cut her out and played "pretend" with the figures. I showed Eva, Tami, and Katy how to draw clothes for them.

Eva scoffed, "What a baby, still playing with paper dolls!"

"It's not the same thing," I protested. "I use them to design clothes. See?"

"Call it what you want. Come on, guys," she said and walked away with Tami and Katy.

I continued adding wardrobes and then created scenarios for Brenda. In the comic strip, she had a weird boyfriend named Basil with an eye patch. An eye patch? Pirates wore those, not a partner for heroines. I drew new boyfriends—"tall, dark, and handsome"—who escorted her to balls and grand dinners at palaces. For each occasion, I designed a new gown, brilliantly studded with jewels, and a new tiara. Less often I designed working clothes, suits, and plain dresses for her daily job at the news office. Even years later, I found myself creating imaginary outfits for Brenda. Sometimes I sketched a blouse or dress, and my mother drafted a pattern for me. My senior-prom dress was one such creation: a glorious ombré lavender chiffon gown.

And then there were weekly movies in the mess hall. Sometimes we walked to the next block, 9K, sometimes to our own. We screamed, as expected of us, when Frank Sinatra or Bing Crosby crooned "I'll Be Around" and "White Christmas," then giggled in embarrassment, hoping we hadn't been too loud. I waited and wished fervently for the newly released *Lassie Come Home* with Elizabeth Taylor, but it never showed. I swirled with Fred Astaire and Ginger Rogers and tap-danced with Ann Miller and Eleanor Powell. I escaped into their fantasy lives for two hours, and that memory sparkled into the next day.

Unlike summer's eruption, fall crept in day by day. The sagebrush clung to its dusty gray color but became more brittle. The moths, mosquitoes, and rattlers retreated. We folded and stored the mosquito nets. The jackrabbits, though, continued to hop nervously to the fence for the cook's scraps.

The coyotes howled less urgently; perhaps they migrated south. I was told that coyotes, too, fed on the food by the fence but were stealthier.

"They eat babies, too," Eva told me. "When a girl gets pregnant and doesn't want the baby, she leaves it out there, and by morning—just like that—it's gone."

I knew she was lying. "My mother told me those babies were left at churches and hospitals."

"I've seen their bones. I can show you."

So Eva and I walked along the barbed-wire fence, and—sure enough—we found some tiny bones, but they looked like chicken legs and breast bones to me, remnants of mess garbage.

"See," Eva pointed to the fragments.

"Come on; anyone can see they're not human bones," I said.

"How do you know? You ever see real human ones?"

She had a point, but I didn't see any reason to draw this discussion out. I pretended to be interested in the unusual cloud formations and changed the subject.

•

Then school started once more, and I was a sixth-grader. Mrs. Bender was our teacher again, and Mr. Hinman continued as music director. My brother joined the Troop 179 Boy Scouts and learned to play the trumpet so he could join the Bugle Corps. He practiced diligently. He went to socials, forbidden to sixth- and seventh-graders. My friends and I practiced the jitterbug and the two-step so we wouldn't look like fools when we were finally invited to these dances. We listened with pitcher ears as the older girls gossiped and giggled about making out in dark corners and the older boys bragged about the number of willing girls they had kissed.

•

One morning the classroom buzzed with gossip: Sumi's brother, who had "itchy feet," had been caught hiding behind a building in Granada and brought back to camp. Several young men had attempted prior escapes from camp, but all had been caught. Their punishment was working at a menial job and attending special rehab classes. I wasn't sure what they were taught—more obedience?

I was taken aback that Sumi's brother had tried to escape and find his way alone back to California. He was only several years older than Sumi, and although I didn't know the family well, it seemed to be cohesive and caring. After all, it was Sumi's father who had found his way to our classroom to save us in that dust storm and had led students safely home. I wished I had such a heroic father.

However, a loving family was, perhaps, not the issue. This young man had fled toward freedom beyond the barbed wire with the same yearning that I had. Yes, I wanted to flee, too, but he had done it, whereas I only thought about it. He was brave enough to try, only to be branded "bad." I secretly applauded him, and when Sumi returned to school the next day, I intended to confess my feelings to her. However, as soon as she stepped in the door, the students suddenly became busy at their desks, and no one spoke to her, as if she had conspired with her brother. This made no sense, but I timidly followed the pack. In time we forgot about the incident, and it seemed too late to bring it up again. Or perhaps it was cowardice on my part.

BLUE SKIES, NOTHIN' BUT

Once I found myself sitting across from my brother at breakfast. He was carefully scraping minute flakes of butter from the rock-hard slab in front of us. I watched as he grazed a tiny bit onto his knife and patted it onto his now-cold toast…over and over, so patiently, so carefully, until he had covered the surface with an even coat of butter. I watched, amazed. Everyone else either skipped the butter—too much trouble—or laid great uneven hunks on top of the toast like pebbles.

"Why'd you do that?" I asked.

"To butter my toast, dummy. But doesn't it look good?" Sumiya grinned proudly.

PARADISE LOST, WATERCOLOR, 22 BY 30 INCHES.
In a nostalgic mood, I painted some of the things I missed in camp: the ocean, fresh oranges, palm trees, ice cream, and butterflies. The two antique dolls represent my lost childhood; they were rescued from a thrift store.

A photo of the Amache Elementary School seventh-grade class taken
in front of the high school. I am in the middle row and am the only girl with glasses.

I persisted, "You could wait until the butter gets soft, then spread it. Look at all the time it took you to do that. Everyone's almost finished except for you."

"So?" He bit into a corner of the toast and smacked his lips.

And, yes, I felt a strange sort of envy. My brother was leisurely enjoying this communal breakfast as if he were dining in an elegant restaurant. I finished my glass of milk and left him alone to savor his buttered toast.

Complaints about the food were rampant—little ones like the frozen butter to major ones like inedible gristly meat, looking more like rubber bands than food, or coffee, sometimes made from barley, with burnt grounds clumped at the bottom of the cup. But I didn't mind that much. My mother was not the best of cooks, although she always concerned herself with nutrition and "good-o health," so we ate balanced meals but never anything extraordinary. The fresh vegetables, steadily supplied from her garden, were served plain—boiled with a touch of salt.

I had my first taste of squid at Amache, and while my friends squealed, "Oh, yuk, look at the suckers on the tentacles," I savored these morsels simmered in soy sauce and gladly accepted Tami's portion. Another new item to me was corn fritters dripping in fat, probably heart-stopping lard. They were crunchy and chewy at the same time, a minor miracle.

To supplement our diet, my mother ordered Horlicks' malted milk and Ovaltine from Monkey Ward. They both had strange aftertastes, but my brother and I drank them because they were "good for us." The labels assured us that we'd have strong bones. No one understood about lactose intolerance in those years, so I recall unexplainable squeezing gut pains and the runs after some meals. My mother told me it was due to eating too fast. "Chew your food thirty times before you swallow," she'd say as I dashed for the bathroom.

The older kids were always harping about the quantity, rather than the quality, of the meals, and they rushed off to other mess halls for another meal, although Sumiya denied this. However, I remember him and his friends gossiping about checking out "the chicks" at various mess halls, so perhaps ogling was the point, not food.

And the way we had to eat! Noisy pipe signals three times a day, rain or shine, snow or gale. Because those summoning bells were also used for emergency call-ups—like volunteer fire squads, special meetings, and weather warnings—their sound was tinged with a sense of danger. Mealtime rituals disintegrated. I sat with my friends, not my parents; my parents sat with their friends, Dad with his, Mom with hers. There was no "fun dinner talk," and the assault of so many people noisily jabbering disordered my mind.

The government decreed that the camps had to become self-sustaining so that funds could be diverted to "the war effort." I wasn't sure what that meant, but I assumed the idea was that the money saved on trucking in foodstuffs could be spent on "military-imposed priorities," as Mrs. Bender put it. Probably that meant tanks, machine guns, and fighter planes. We also heard that outside people resented that the evacuees were given rationed foods—sugar, coffee, lard, cheese, butter, canned milk, and jam—in unlimited wasteful quantities. They felt that it was unfair to the "patriotic" Americans that the enemy—that was us—got treated so well. Perhaps the government was mollifying the public.

Because half the people in Amache had come from rural areas, these farmers established themselves as leaders of this new initiative, and the acreage north of Amache flourished and provided the camp with much of its vegetables, meat, and dairy products. By the following year, the surrounding towns coveted the cattle and pigs the farmers had raised, so calves and piglets were gifted to the townships around us. The farmers and workers seemed happy to be involved in labor that the people appreciated. I remember the rich aroma and taste of the first tomato from those fields. I let the juice dribble down my chin.

My mother said these farmers had "the magic touch." She wistfully repeated, "I wish I had that magic touch."

I corrected her: "It's a 'green thumb.'"

"Yes, but magic touch is better."

"Magic touch it is," I agreed.

•

The children were encouraged to grow victory gardens. Our sixth-grade class had a plot we named Bender's Farm about two miles outside of camp.

One sweltering day our class walked there. I didn't share my mother's enthusiasm for gardening—you got all that gunk beneath your nails—but I enjoyed the outing because we were free, beyond the barbed wire. Even the air smelled fresher. It seemed lighter, easier to breathe. I took deep breaths.

"Let's see if the girls can pull more weeds than the boys today," Mrs. Bender encouraged.

I squatted by the budding radish plants but felt woozy, so I sank to my knees and punched at the weeds with the ineffectual stick that substituted for a tool. Suddenly, I felt nauseated and sought shade under a wagon.

"Hey, Mrs. Bender, no fair; Yuriko's not working," someone called out.

"Yes, of course, let's all sit down for a while," Mrs. Bender said. She produced a large jug of water, and we took turns drinking from two cups.

An hour later, I felt no better. We started back to Amache. We had only walked a few minutes when I knew I couldn't take another step.

"I'm going to faint," I whispered to the girl next to me.

"Sure, go ahead," she laughed.

I did.

When I came to, Mrs. Bender was worriedly bending over me and waving the other students away. She hailed a truck, and I found myself lying next to sacks of potatoes on a bumpy ride back to camp. At the hospital, the doctor took a cursory look and diagnosed measles. He sent me home with a quarantine notice to put on the door.

When I returned to school a week later, I discovered I had introduced measles to the class. Maybe it was the communal drinking cup.

•

Snow cones were a Sunday treat at Amache. We scraped small blocks of ice with Japanese ice shavers, one of which was ours. Had my mother packed that as an afterthought? A whim? The ice shaver was coveted here. In the blazing sun, we carried it to the rec room at the end of the laundry room.

Shhh, shhh, the blade sang, and beneath it slivers of white flakes mounded into bowls. We poured on red or green Kool-Aid and reveled in our Sunday specials. On particularly windy days, we nicknamed them "dusties" because if we didn't eat them quickly, we found ourselves crunching a mixture of sand and ice. The best part was the soupy cold at the bottom. We slurped and licked and ended up with red or green lips and tongues. We laughed at each other's remarkable faces.

Some years later—when my granddaughter Autumn was nine—I brought out our new automatic Snow-Cone machine (superdeluxe, guaranteed to produce fine slivers of ice) to make snow cones for us. I set it on "fine texture," added ice cubes, and watched as chunks of unevenly crushed ice clinked into the dish. Perhaps I was doing something wrong. I tried again

Our ice shaver. Shaved ice was a special summer treat at the camp.
It was sweetened with Kool-Aid.

with the same result. Autumn chose green syrup to pour over her portion. She bit into the ice. Her expression said "disappointing."

Then I remembered the antique ice shaver tucked away on a shelf, saved as a tribute to my mother's odd foresight. We froze a block of ice and made snow cones the old-fashioned way.

"Look, Autumn, this works better than the machine," I told her. Autumn and I both had big grins on our faces as we savored the syrup at the bottom. It was sweet and icy, the way I remembered it many years before.

•

A sudden rainstorm deluged the camp in July. Without warning the sky—clear and blue one minute—gathered huge angry clouds with black under-bellies. The raindrops pelted the ground and pocked the dry sand, and within seconds the rain was falling in sheets. I sprinted for cover beneath the roof of a tiny porch between two rooms and watched, fascinated, as the water poured around my feet and was momentarily dammed by the doors on either side of me. Suddenly, the doors burst open, and the churning water, roiling with mud, flooded the rooms.

From within people screamed, "What's happening!?" "Oh, lordy." "Someone help!" An old woman sloshed toward me from one room. "What's happening? Who are you? What did you do?" She screeched in panic.

From the other door, a young man shouted, "My God, you stupid kid. What have you done?"

I could only stand between them, dumbfounded. When I found my voice, I cried, "It's the rain. It's the storm, not me," and picked my feet out of the mud. "Can't you see? Can't you hear the thunder? You're the stupid one, not me." Before he could figure out who I was, I slogged to the pathway and faced the blinding rain. I had been on my way home from summer class and was clutching my tonette and a sheet of now illegible music.

I headed for the dim outline of the laundry room. Dripping wet, but sheltered, I stood by the window listening to the raging storm. Thunder crashed above my head. Rain pelted the window. I felt as if I had been flung into violent ocean waves. Then—as if a conductor had swung down his baton for the finale—the rain faltered, and the sun peeked out, sending tentative rays through the bloated clouds.

"What was that all about?" someone behind me asked.

"Flash flood," a man answered.

The rain had lasted only about fifteen or twenty minutes, but what a torrential one it was. Rivulets coursed down between the barracks. Water dripped eagerly off the eaves, then steamed up in a fog. The barracks appeared to be smoldering from an aborted fire.

When I got home, my mother was on her way to check on Obah-san and Ojii-san. Did I want to come along?

Actually, no, but I told her I'd follow in a few minutes.

When I started up the hill toward Barrack 11F, I saw that the blocks at the south edge of camp had caught the brunt of the storm. The water—unimpeded by other structures—had slammed into the Block 12 barracks, and the debris and mud it carried had plastered the barracks almost to the windows. People were already shoveling and scraping the mud and ooze away.

I hesitated at my grandparents' door, then turned back down the slope. Their entrance was unscathed, and I didn't have anything to say to them anyway.

●

The highlight of the summer was the Obon Festival. We danced to honor our ancestors, who blessed us from heaven. When I was five or six, my mother had made me a blue silk kimono for the occasion.

"It's too tight. I can't breathe," I complained. An obi pushed up against my chest like a vise.

"Stand still. I need to tie the bow."

"I can't. I can't."

"No butsu butsu. Don't complain."

I burst into tears. *I was going to die from suffocation. They'd be sorry. In my kimono with this tight obi bound around me, I'd lie in my coffin, and people would cry and wonder why I had to die like this. "So young," they'd say. Sob, sob.*

Eventually my mother relented. She substituted a simple soft sash and let the ends dangle. What a relief! But yet to come was the trial of the Obon dance. I tried to keep pace with the drums and flute: step, step, back; step, step, back.

Don, don, chin. Don, don, chin.

I concentrated, but it was hard when my toes were imprisoned in the two-toed *tabi* and stiff, cardboardlike *zori.* I stumbled over my own feet.

Kachi, kachi, don. Kachi, kachi, don.

I circled with the dancers, eying the girl in front of me, hoping she remembered the steps. We danced and appeased the dead and wished them peace.

Don, don, chin. Don, don, chin.

At Amache at the bottom of the trunk, I found my two silk kimonos— one cobalt blue, the other ruby red. I had hoped to wear them at the Obon dance, but I had grown taller, and when I tried them on, they only reached midcalf, so we ordered a white-and-blue cotton print and made new ones: a kimono for me, and another for my mother.

"These aren't kimonos," my mother explained. "These are *yukata. Momen,* cotton, for summer. Much easier to wash."

There, too, at the bottom of the trunk was the tiny brocaded purse to tuck into the obi. It was ornamented by miniature bells that tinkled, hardly making a sound. I always wondered what the sheets of tidily folded rice paper inside were for. "Just padding, I think," my mother said. I once pulled the paper out and checked for writing, but there was none. Beside the purse lay my celluloid headband, twisted red and white, adorned with a huge bow and gold wire. We used neither in camp. The headband was too babyish, the purse too treasured to risk losing.

"We look like sisters," my mother said when we donned our identical yukata. "Maybe Sumiye would look like you. Poor thing," she added, remembering her dead sister. "I wish I had a picture of her. She's only in my head. We'll dance for her tonight."

As we approached the dance grounds, I heard a drumbeat. The sound was odd, and I soon saw why. A man was pounding the bass drum from the high-school orchestra. Not as resonant as a *taiko,* it was meant for marching, not dancing. But in camp we made do. A woman was warming up a *fue,* a Japanese flute. It was sweeter than the ones I had heard in the city.

The music drifted into the vast emptiness and faded gently…so gently, spiraling into the hollow spaces above. This music would surely tremble into the heavens, touch souls, and soothe troubled ghosts still haunting us. *Ooouue…e…yoh,* it lamented.

We danced in the desert, kicking up puffs of dust…step, step, back…step, step, back. We danced for Sumiye. We danced for our ancestors. We danced for Buddha. We danced for ourselves.

Ban, ban. Ban, ban.

Oooouuue…eeee.

The fue conjured up scenes that drifted in and out of my mind like dreams: a line of ancient court figures…white and crimson robes swaying in a spring breeze, cherry blossoms fluttering down around them. A maiden—her long black hair tied primly behind her neck—reading a scroll from her lover. An old man and woman holding hands on a bench, staring at the rippling water at the edge of a pond. A stoic *ronin,* a samurai with no master, slicing the air in slow motion with a whirling blade.

But most vividly, the plaintive sound reminded me of a bedtime story that my mother often read to me and my brother. In medieval Japan, a high-born woman with her two children, Anju and Zushio, along with their maid, are searching for her exiled husband. They make inquiries at a sea-shore town, but no one has any information. Some vagabonds, pretending kindness, kidnap them. The children watch in horror as the women are forced onto a boat. An evil man enslaves the children, but Zushio escapes, clutching a small Buddhist statue that Anju hid on herself and gives now to Zushio with her blessing. Zushio, befriended by a priest, becomes a powerful lord. He rescues Anju, and they search for their mother. They find her—blind and destitute—but because of her children's faith, she regains her sight. There is a joyful reunion.

Tears in her eyes, my mother said, "Zushio had faith. He believed in the amulet that he always carried. You must have faith, Yuriko, Sumiya. If I get lost, you must look for me."

Ban, ban.

Ooouue…e…yoh.

Ban, ban.

Beautiful Anju-hime. Mighty Zushio. I held fast to the magic story swirling in my head. *Yes, if my mother got lost, I would look for her. Of course, I would look for her. I would have faith. I would believe in Buddha.*

Japanese lanterns bobbed on a string, stirred by a faint breeze. Long banners trailed from poles. I saw my mother sitting on the sidelines, fanning herself with an *uchiwa.* She appeared content. After years of hardship—the ordeals of terrible upheavals—this desert exile seemed the least-promising arena for a peaceful life. And yet here my mother sat, far from Japan, the country she kept yearning for, with a serene expression on her face that I seldom saw. Fate was unpredictable. My mother focused on a single karmic thread—the inevitability of her unlucky debts adding up from lives past—but now maybe the favorable ones were crowding out the bad ones.

I walked to her side. "I found you," I said.

My father's mandolin banjo with the sheet music for "Blue Skies."

My mother had brought my father's mandolin banjo to camp. She strummed and sang popular tunes of the day in a sweet, but slightly off-tune, voice: "Blue Skies," "Melancholy Baby," "Yes, Sir! That's My Baby." I had heard these songs for years, but now the incongruity of popular American songs in a prison camp suddenly struck me as hilarious.

"What's so funny?" my mother asked, and without waiting for an answer, she continued singing: "Blue skies, smiling at me. Nothing but blue skies do I see. Bluebirds singing a song. Nothing but bluebirds all day long. Never saw the sun shining so bright…"

I stopped laughing and watched her, so intent and serious as if the melody could somehow force bluebirds to appear and cheerfully scoot away the somber surroundings.

"Never saw things going so right," she continued.

"Going so right?" Was she aware of what she was singing? But perhaps for her, the days may have been going so right. I had witnessed her calm demeanor on Obon night, after all. Yes, blue skies might be smiling at her.

Two Dollars Due

Piano recitals came in different packages—simple and brief or perhaps formal with us wearing gowns or kimonos—but they were, most of all, scary. My first recital was a disaster. I was eight. The piece was only two pages, but I forgot the notes leading to the second page and repeated the phrase three times, hoping I'd remember what came next. I didn't. I had begun a fourth time when Miss Wilker whispered, "Skip that and go on to the next page." I stopped playing. "Start over," she whispered again. I did. I stumbled on the same phrase. "We'll try again a little later," Miss Wilker told the audience. I returned, ashamed, to my seat.

"You were so pretty in your new dress," Miss Wilker said tactfully after the program. Then she turned to my mother and tried to ease her discomfort: "You are such a talented seamstress, Mrs. Nakai."

My mother made a slight bow and apologized. "I'm sorry. Yuriko will practice harder, Miss Wilker."

I had embarrassed them both. A stone settled in my stomach, and I didn't know what to say.

When we got home, my mother adjusted the clock squarely in front of me atop the piano. "Half hour," she said.

I learned then and there that piano recitals were performances to show off how much you had learned—how well you could memorize, note by note, what a composer had written on some staffs. Oh, yes, of course, when you were better or already some genius, you could interpret, but until then you had to mind those p's and f's—pianissimos and fortes, crescendos and ritards. If you forgot the notes, you had to practice and memorize some more. The recitals were productions for the benefit of parents who had paid all that money so that their children could be cultured. Or act one up on the other children.

Mary Watanabe's piano students at Amache in 1945. I am in the top row on the right end.
I helped tutor several of the beginning students.

I could do that. I practiced for exactly thirty minutes and then ran out to play with my friends. It was not until many years later—when my mother began piano and organ lessons late in life—that I realized that she had an innate love for music. She really hadn't cared if I missed a few notes—she hit quite a few wrong ones herself—or whether I performed in a recital or not.

•

Miss Mary Watanabe, the piano instructor at Amache, never spoke about beauty in music but insisted on pretty titles for her recitals, as if that would help the students take themselves more seriously.

"'From Bud to Blossom.' So appropriate, don't you think?" she asked. "Little buds, these new students, and now they've blossomed."

It sounded corny to me. The printed programs of the recitals at the Los Angeles Conservatory were straightforward and more honest somehow, with just the word "Recital" and the date on the cover.

Now at Amache, the tables had turned; I was no longer a child, seated before that intimidating instrument in an auditorium of strangers. Instead, for this final recital, I sat at the rear, furtively eying the parents. Miss Watanabe had asked me to tutor some of the beginners, and this was my initiation program as a teacher. I hoped fervently that I had instilled beauty into the hearts of those seven-year-old girls and that they could play with love, not fear.

"You know," one of the parents said after the program, "if we hadn't come to Amache, Alice would probably never have had piano lessons. We thought music was a frill. Strange, isn't it, how things turn out? We want to thank you and Miss Watanabe."

Yes, it was strange. In Los Angeles, my mother had insisted on my lessons. She had bought an old upright piano, lovingly polished it, and crocheted an elaborate doily for its top. She had put aside money for lessons and whatever new music Miss Wilker brought. She had sacrificed so that music would always be a part of my life.

Late one night I had heard my mother and father arguing. It seemed to be about the petty cash for my piano lessons. My father had found and spent it. Long after my father stormed out the door, I heard my mother rustling about. At my weekly lesson, my mother handed Miss Wilker the two dollars due.

•

By the third year in Amache, it became hard to remember that life had ever been any different. Living in a single room in a barrack in a barren desert, eating meals in a noisy communal mess hall, attending school and church in yet-another common barrack, interacting only with other Japanese, washing and bathing in a separate building, shopping for necessary commodities with government coupons at a canteen—all the while supervised and watched by Caucasians and some recruited Japanese police, those *inu*—this life began to feel normal, and yet I knew it wasn't. I was reminded over and over that real life was outside.

The soldiers disappeared from the towers sometime in 1944. Tami and I investigated one. The view was boring—gray roofs staggered in rows, and the gray-green sage and tumbleweeds rolled to the horizon. I looked toward Kansas, desperately straining to see a contrasting landscape, a shift in color or shape to indicate that magical place I had longed for all these years. There was none. The inside melted seamlessly into the outside.

Rumors began to circulate that a corps of bachelor Issei men were determined to live out their lives in camp, that they had sworn never to move again. They would have to be dragged away. They would tie themselves to their beds and bar their doors. They had nothing to return to, and here they had food to eat and a bed. Although meager, it was enough. They claimed that when they had arrived in America, their lives had been just as difficult, but, at least in camp, they didn't have to work from dawn to dusk pounding spikes into the railroad tracks or wash other people's clothes in a tub with water boiled on a fire. The golden lives they had dreamed of had never materialized. The government had effectively crushed what little they had built in America, and they felt that it was their due to be taken care of until they died. They didn't have the will to start all over.

My mother thought they were justified. "Of course they must be allowed to stay here. Look what the government did to them, to us," she said. "We should all revolt and stay here."

My father called them "goof-offs," *noroi namakes.*

Then my mother said thoughtfully, "No, I guess our family must go outside because I want Sumiya and Yuriko to get an education. But, yes, we must allow the old men to live out their lives here."

My father seemed genuinely horrified. "What are you saying? *Baka* thoughts. Don't you know you can still get in trouble for siding with these men? You know they will get thrown out on their asses."

In the end, the holdouts gave in, resigning themselves to the inevitable. *Shikataganai.* Only one man had to be dragged out of camp by force.

●

The war was nearing its end, and the government had the massive task of dismantling the internment camps. To shift public opinion about us, the government began circulating news articles and radio broadcasts about the "efficient, hard-working, intelligent" Japanese. Suddenly, we were "law-abiding citizens" who were eager to return to a "normal life" after our chastening stay in the comfortable camps. They urged us to leave as soon as possible, to apply for jobs before the soldiers returned and glutted the market. "Hurry," they prodded, "for your own sakes." "Leave so we can close the centers and shove this black chapter into oblivion." That's how some internees interpreted the injunction.

The about-face didn't surprise my father. "I knew the end would be like this. We are *kuso* when it's convenient for the government and then good guys when they need our cooperation," he said.

The relocation centers had become a financial liability and a source of embarrassment because after the propaganda about sneaky Japanese sabotaging the West Coast, not one incident had been recorded. To the contrary, the Japanese American 100th Infantry Battalion from Hawaii and the 442nd Regimental Combat Team of the United States Army had proven themselves loyal citizens by earning the largest number of citations awarded to any military group. I could hear my mother admonishing me to study three times harder than whites to compensate for my yellowness. Swim uphill farther, harder, to reach the same end. My mother's advice seemed to have infiltrated the entire Nisei ethos.

Families began moving outside, to the East or even back to California, where some encountered notices that the Japanese were not welcome: "No Japs wanted. Keep moving." We heard news about Ku Klux Klan–type groups barring us from returning home. Notices of even more jobs appeared in the semiweekly newsletter, "The Granada Pioneer," and on all manner of walls, even in our schools: Gardeners for families and estates, carpenters and construction workers for Quaker Oats Ordnance, pottery workers, domestics, secretaries, and even an occasional advertisement for a physician or teacher. Although the pay was low—from seventy cents an hour to sixty to a hundred dollars a month, it was more than the twelve or nineteen dollars per month in camp salaries. Chicago seemed to be the most glamorous and desirable place to go: a big city. Sophisticated. A glittering metropolis that held unlimited possibilities. My father made a tentative foray there, and for weeks we waited for news that he had found a job and a place for us to move.

"It's not a good place," he said when he returned. "Dangerous city. Full of gangsters. Apartments cost more than I can make. If I had extra money to grease palms, maybe it would be possible."

I didn't understand, then, how so many families were able to move there, including Tami's large family. Both my mother and I protested, but my father wouldn't listen.

My father drifted back and forth from camp to the latest great-job tip. As men sought outside work, women took over as cooks, carpenters, drivers, electricians…every job left behind. My mother began sewing clothes for people for a small fee.

When V-E Day was announced on May 8, 1945, we were told the war would end soon, but it dragged on through the summer. We endured another season of sweltering heat, but this time the days were infused with worry about our future. Our primary concern was "Where? Where could we go?" My mother urged my father to try harder, to find a destination, an apartment, anything. "What does your Daddy expect us to do—sleep in the street?" she asked us in frustration. She offered to accompany him on his search, but my father quickly vetoed the suggestion: "What can you do? You're only a woman."

Adding to our anxiety was news that some homes of families who had returned to California had been burned and warning shots blasted into other homes. The War Relocation Authority offered no help—they had been founded only to move the Japanese enemy into the camps, not return them home. The responsibility belonged to the states, they claimed, not the United States government.

On August 6, 1945, Hiroshima was obliterated by the atom bomb. We began our plans in earnest for yet-another relocation with a kind of desperation. Where could we go? We had no home in Los Angeles. My father had not found us a place.

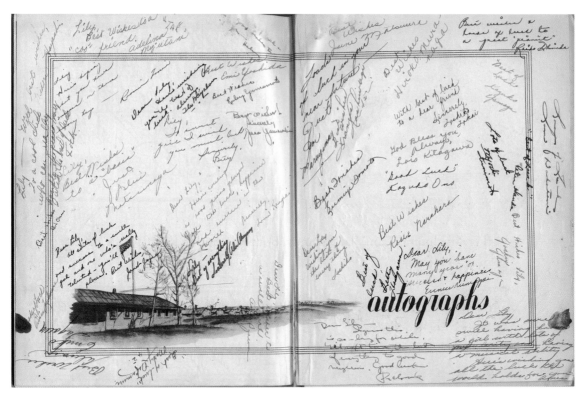

The autographs in my copy of the Onlooker, the Amache school yearbook.

Then a miracle arrived in the mail. Mr. and Mrs. Harrington sent my parents a check, enough money for a down payment on a small house. My mother held the envelope to her chest for a long time. But, again, came that nagging question: where? My Aunt Frances and her husband were in Salt Lake City, and my mother asked if they could locate a place. A few weeks later, they had good news: a house was available. "Small and a little run-down, but after all…," they wrote. They had asked the neighbors (a tacit rule) if they would accept a Japanese family, and they had all agreed.

Talking and thinking about the outside was one thing; facing the reality was another. Part of me was excited and eager to take flight, to rid myself of this drab place, but the other part was scared and uncertain. I had spent almost a third of my life in wartime camps. People around me spoke of getting a real life, but this was my real life. I saw what I saw—the barrack home, the mess hall, the friends I had made—and heard what I heard—the mess bell, the desert winds, the coyotes. I smelled and tasted, I touched the world surrounding me.

This was my real world. What was this other real world that the adults spoke about? What did these older, more experienced people know about realness that I didn't? Life was an illusion, a dream, the priest told us. That was weird. What, then, were my dreams within this dream life?

"Don't worry. We'll be okay," my mother assured me. "I will take care of you. You and Sumiya."

One activity of those final weeks was signing the *Onlooker,* the school yearbook, which in 1945 included seventh grade: "Dear Lily, it was swell knowing such a swell gal." We scribbled, "Good luck in the future. May we meet again in better conditions." "Loads of luck" and "best wishes" filled my book. Everyone and everything was "cool" and "swell": "cool gals; cool guys." We were no longer girls and boys but "swell kids," "swell gals." I didn't know if my future would be lucky or cool or swell.

I was compelled to do something I had not done before—walk around the perimeter of the camp. Bid a final farewell to Amache. Although the lower-numbered blocks were only a mile away, I had never spent much time there— just a few visits to friends' barracks and the original "store" at Block 6F. When a bigger co-op was built near the high school, I had no need to hike down to that area.

I began a circular route by going up the slight rise, that is, south toward the Number-11 Blocks. For years I had been convinced that up was north. Mrs. Bender taught us to read maps that way. But here it was the opposite. So I started south and peeked into the Christian church at the end of Block 10H, a rec room converted into a place of worship. The door was open. It looked like our Buddhist Church except for the large picture of Jesus, his head leaning sideways, eyes closed, with a golden halo radiating light around him. I was glad he wasn't nailed to a cross, bleeding and dying. I sang my Jesus song to him: "Jesus loves me; this I know, for the Bible tells me so."

I walked to the corner of the camp and peered into the faded sagebrush and dusty gold rabbitbrush reaching toward New Mexico, or maybe it was the Oklahoma panhandle. Then there was the other Buddhist Church at the very southern end of camp with a guard tower standing benignly a short distance away. There wasn't a golden altar, but someone had been there recently. A thin spiral of smoke threaded toward the ceiling from sticks of incense. I offered a simple prayer: *"Namu amida butsu;* I put my faith in Buddha."

Nearby was the barrack where someone had yelled at me and called me stupid because the flash-flood waters had swept into his room. For a second, I hesitated and wondered, "Shall I knock and ask, 'Remember me'?" It seemed like a ridiculous idea. I quickly slipped by.

A few blocks more and there it was, the cemetery. Some neatly carved headstones stood guard over a few of the graves. A handful of grasshoppers played hopscotch through the scrubby weeds. How sad to end one's life in a concentration camp! I repeated the only thing possible, "Rest in peace," or as I had heard my mother say, *"Yasurakani yasume."*

An American flag stood a few barracks to the north—the Boy Scouts' office. I remembered watching my brother's troop practicing to lead an honor guard and marching smartly behind a waving flag, but it was at the high school, not here. Some boys cracked rude remarks: "Flat-foot floozies with the floy, floy," "pansies," "fairies," "maybe they have skirts under their pants." I was relieved that the scouts couldn't hear them.

I ambled toward a jumble of structures at the north end of camp, the "ad" buildings, the administration quarters where the mostly Caucasian personnel worked. Barbed wire stretched between them and our barracks. I skirted the Number-6 Blocks, walking as if I needed to escape, uncomfortable at being somewhere I didn't belong. This was foreign territory.

I headed east again. The hospital presented itself, planted firmly, rebuffing the sand and dust swirling in puffs against it. A permanent core of custodians constantly swept and mopped, trying to keep pace with the onslaught, but they could never win. As I peered down the white hallway, a man was on his hands and knees scrubbing arcs of soapy water on the floor. He meekly smiled and motioned me to cross his clean floor. I smiled back, shook my head no, and hastily retreated.

Brooches created from scrap wood by Mr. Satomura at Amache.

Heading back to Block 9L, I paused at the guard tower and imagined the soldier who had reached out for my bleeding hand. I again saw my father running toward us, moving as fast as I've ever seen him, swearing, "Sonofa-bitch, get away from her," grabbing my hand, and not letting go. His hand, tough as leather, held on.

That same day Mr. Satomura presented me with a brooch inscribed Yuriko that he had carved from the bark of a tree. "Something to remember me and Amache by," he said. Mr. Satomura was my father's friend, not mine. He acknowledged me mostly with short nods and brief hellos. Sometimes I hated him because he and my father drank so much together, and I blamed him for all those hours when my father could have been clear headed and with me or our family. No, that wasn't the truth. My father drank of his own free will, and Mr. Satomura was merely his drinking buddy. I still hated him sometimes. Nevertheless, I had a catch in my throat when I thanked him. "We'll come see you one day," I answered.

This is the final photo of me at Amache. My father planted the elm tree
a few months after our arrival in 1942.

•

My father returned to help with the final move. The last night in Amache
felt eerily like the first. Both times I was on the verge of a strange new life.
The future was vague, unknown. I was filled with anxiety and turmoil. It
was September. We were still a family of four—the same people but vastly
different inside from the four who had arrived more than three years earlier.
My brother, Sumiya, had transformed from a boy to a tall, "cool" teenager
nicknamed Semi. He distanced himself from all of us in an attempt to find
the man emerging from within.

My father had disappeared both physically and mentally. His depression
had surfaced, and even when he joined us in camp, his thoughts escaped

A group photo of the Block 9L residents in 1945.

beyond our reach. Life within the camp was unbearable to him, but in all his forays beyond the barbed wire, he had found life even less welcoming. He blamed his parents and their gross neglect. He blamed his wife for being inattentive to his needs but was unable to articulate what those might be. He blamed the government for uprooting what small gains he had made before the war. He may have even blamed my brother and me for keeping him tied down. Then, of course, he blamed himself for the failures of his life, for choosing those wrong paths over and over again. I felt that he had given up. Any adversity would be too great for him.

My mother, on the other hand, had challenged these harsh surroundings and emerged newly focused. She had found a life independent of her husband and was determined to pursue her new future. She had plans of opening a sewing school in Salt Lake City, of establishing a dressmaking shop, of returning to school to learn more English, and, most of all, of making sure that her children were properly educated.

And I, I was stumbling into the teen years, aware that there would be greater obstacles than practicing on an out-of-tune piano in a barrack. I was about to rejoin the regular American school system, sidewalks and streetcars, grocery stores and movie houses. I knew that the outside—the people— could be a hostile place, that I was still considered part of the enemy, only now—according to government assessment—we were hardworking and diligent, not sneaky and yellow bellied. I was awestruck by what might lie beyond that horizon but fearful of that same unknown.

Early the next morning, we hitched a ride on a truck to Granada. My father gripped his cardboard suitcase and looked away from the camp, but I stared and stared at the retreating barracks and then at the single dusty road leading to the outside.

"Good-bye, Amache," I whispered.

BLUE LOTUS, WATERCOLOR, 22 BY 30 INCHES.
My mother clutches a bouquet of red peonies as an offering to my father. Buddhist angels
dropping blue lotus flowers console her. The blue lotus is a Buddhist symbol.
It thrives even in muddy waters.

Epilogue

The Bow

THE BOW

I met Uncle Zentatsu in 1980. I worried about the way to greet him. One's depth of bow depends on social status. The lower the status, the lower the bow, showing deference to the more exalted person. Should I bow to my waist? Bow at all? Perhaps shake hands Western style? My mother had no advice: "Do what you want. He knows you don't know proper Japanese manners." So do I appear like a bumbling American?

The local train jerked and rattled and stopped at every tiny hamlet and town as it chugged along the narrow tracks, sometimes hugging the hillside only an arm's length away from my window. Most of the passengers were asleep, heads bouncing like Bobbleheads. A half hour later, we were just ten miles out of Hiroshima. Twenty more to Kajita, our destination. *Gatan, goton. Gatan, goton.*

"What shall I call him...*ojisan?* Uncle? Iwatake-san?" I asked my mother again.

"Anything. He won't care." Why was my mother being so nonchalant? She who was always repeating—like a needle stuck on a record—about "the way it was supposed to be"? She who carried on about being correct, doing the proper thing?

Gatan, goton; gatan, goton. Another half hour, another ten miles.

"We'll visit my mother's grave at the Kounu Temple, too," my mother said. "Poor mother, poor Sumiye. Both of them; we'll visit both of them."

TWO FACES OF HIROSHIMA, WATERCOLOR, 22 BY 30 INCHES.
Modern high-rise buildings sprout in Hiroshima today, displacing older traditional homes.
My mother didn't recognize this Hiroshima.

My Uncle Zentatsu Iwatake in his ordination robes
when he became a Zen Buddhist priest, probably about 1945.

The ashes of her mother and her little sister, Sumiye, were buried behind the temple where her father had presided and preached. "We must do this soon because the government is building a dam, and the temple and their graves will be under water in a few years," she said solemnly.

Thirty minutes later, we chugged into Kounu station, the one before Kajita.

"So we're visiting the graves before seeing Uncle?" I asked.

"No, we'll come back. There's no train station at Kajita because it's an insignificant place. We'll have to walk from here or take a taxi there."

"Walk? With our luggage? No way!"

But it was the way. We stepped off the train and looked about. There was no taxi in sight. The station master informed us that we could telephone

My Uncle Zentatsu in 1980, when my mother and I returned to Japan to visit him.

the sometimes-on-and-sometimes-off taximan and he might or might not be available. We phoned. He was.

During the short ride to my uncle's house, I fretted more about that initial bow.

"He won't care. He won't notice," my mother reassured me again.

My heart pounded wildly as we approached the temple.

"Ah, here it is, Kajita Oshousan's place," the taxi driver murmured. He bowed very low as we tendered the fare. He bowed again as we began our ascent of the steep stone steps leading to the temple. Why did the steps feel so familiar? I was struck by a sense of déjà vu, but I had never been here.

When we rapped on the *shoji* frame, it slid open almost immediately, and there stood Uncle Iwatake in his crisp *yukata,* his rounded cheeks puffed into a broad smile.

"Ah, *nehsan,* you have finally come," said my uncle, elegantly bowing.

"*Tadaima.*" My mother returned his bow.

Then I witnessed a dramatic transformation in my mother's demeanor—suddenly she was no longer the old lady unable to carry her suitcase up the train-station stairs, who needed help operating the ticket dispensers, who couldn't find her special lavender dress she had packed carefully for this occasion—she instantly became the competent elder sister. She grew taller, and her eyes shone with a maternal glow.

Then I, too, bowed. I bowed and matched his bow—no deeper, no higher. It felt right.

And I understood what my mother had said so many years before in camp: yes, I was American, but I was also Japanese. I, too, had come home. At last.